The Local Job Bank Program:
Performance, Structure, and Direction

The Local Job Bank Program

Performance, Structure, and Direction

Joseph C. Ullman
Purdue University

George P. Huber
University of Wisconsin

Lexington Books
D.C. Heath and Company
Lexington, Massachusetts
Toronto   London

This report was prepared for the Manpower Administration, U.S. Department of Labor, under research contract No. 71-53-70-01 authorized by Title I of the Manpower Development and Training Act. Since contractors performing such work under government sponsorship are encouraged to express their own judgment freely, the report does not necessarily represent the department's official opinion or policy. Moreover, the contractor is solely responsible for the factual accuracy of all material developed in the report.

Library of Congress Cataloging in Publication Data

Ullman, Joseph C.
   The local job bank program.

   "Prepared for the Manpower Administration, U.S. Department of Labor, under research contract no. 71-53-70-01."
   Includes bibliographical references.
   1. Job vacancies—United States—Information services. I. Huber, George P., joint author. II. Title.
HD5724.U52   331.1'28   73-6875
ISBN 0-669-88948-2

Contents

List of Tables and Figures

Preface

This study was conceived while the authors were working in the Manpower Administration during the 1969-70 academic year. During that year, we were supported by the Manpower Administration, the Wisconsin State Employment Service, and the Brookings Institution. The project itself has subsequently been funded by a research contract between the University of Wisconsin and the U.S. Department of Labor, Manpower Administration, Office of Research and Development.

The project received valuable contributions from many persons. Joshua Levine, Division Chief of the Division of Manpower Matching Systems, several members of his staff, and others in USTES aided in the design of the study of Job Bank performance and structure. Howard Rosen, Director of the Office of Research and Development, contributed to the formulation of the study of the effect of feedback on the program administration and direction, and he and Sheridan Maitland of this office arranged for us to meet with key Manpower Administration and USTES officials at various times. Charles Odell, Director of the Office of Systems Support, and Joshua Levine, both administrators of the Job Bank Program, provided the cooperation necessary to study the effect of feedback. Professors Vernon Briggs, Eaton Conant, Dennis Derryck, E.E. Liebhafsky, and David Stevens helped carry out the interview studies in several of the cities. Thomas Hood and Richard Oliver, then graduate students at the University of Wisconsin and now with Arthur Young and Company and the University of Kentucky respectively, carried out much of the data analysis and contributed many excellent ideas in this regard. The University of Wisconsin and Purdue University provided the environment and colleagues that foster and facilitate research efforts such as this. We express our appreciation to our wives for suffering through our long preoccupation with this study and for helpful comments and suggestions for improving the final report.

The usual observation that the authors are solely responsible for remaining errors is especially appropriate in this study. Although we conscientiously endeavored to report the decision-making process as we saw it, we doubt that we always had 20-20 vision. Certainly we did not have all of the data or know all of the pressures affecting those involved in decision-making.

Joseph C. Ullman
George P. Huber

The Local Job Bank Program: Performance, Structure, and Direction

1 Introduction and Overview

The Job Bank Program of the Public Employment Service has been assigned a central role in the federal government's efforts to improve the functioning of our labor-market information system. This book is about the Job Bank Program and an intensive effort to assess its performance, structure, and direction.[1] More explicitly, the research had three goals. The first was to assess the relative goal achievement of Job Banks. The second purpose was to determine the optimal organizational configuration for Job Banks. The third goal was to learn what effect feedback of performance results and recommendations had on program structure and direction.

This initial chapter provides a brief overview of the problems under study and summarizes our findings and conclusions. Chapter 2 describes the Job Bank Program and our approach to studying its performance and the decisions affecting its direction and structure. Chapter 3 contains our findings and recommendations concerning the optimal design configuration for Job Banks and our findings concerning the extent to which Job Banks are achieving their goals. Chapter 4 presents our findings about the effect of feedback on program administrators, and Chapter 5 contains some concluding observations.

The Problems under Study

On the one hand, this study is an assessment of an effort to improve a labor-market information system. On the other hand, the research is an examination of the impact of assessment data on program conduct. This section provides brief background in each of these areas.

Interest in Labor-Market Information

Attempts to improve labor-market information systems have become an explicit part of the federal government's manpower activities.[2] This emphasis results primarily from three considerations: first, there is growing concern that the relation between unemployment and inflation (the Phillips relation) has shifted in such a way that a tolerably stable price level can be achieved only at a cost of unacceptably high unemployment.[3] It is hoped that a more efficient labor-market information system can reduce frictional unemployment and thus help achieve more acceptable overall unemployment levels.

1

The second reason for expanded attention to labor-market information is the increasing awareness that lack of job information is a significant handicap to many present and would-be labor-market participants. Several students of job markets have noted that informal job-information networks do not serve the disadvantaged well, and thus such persons must rely heavily on formal job-information sources.[4] To the extent that formal information systems are ineffective, the information problem of the disadvantaged is compounded. Improved labor-market information systems would help to locate jobs for those who presently lack jobs only for lack of information.

Finally, a key consideration in pending or foreseeable income-maintenance programs relates to the question of finding jobs for program clients. In this regard it seems likely that the Public Employment Service will be called upon to greatly expand and improve the job-market information system associated with Employment Service placement operations.[5]

As can be seen, two of our research purposes were concerned with labor-market information. One was to determine the extent to which local Job Banks are achieving the goals set for the Job Bank Program, particularly the key labor-market information-related goals derived from the above considerations: reduce frictional unemployment, improve service to the disadvantaged, and make Employment Service man-job matching more effective.[6] A second and related purpose of the research was to learn what Job Bank design configuration best meets the goals of the program. To achieve this latter purpose, an analysis was made of the relationship between various organizational and design aspects of Job Banks and several measures of performance.

The Impact of Assessment Results

The research findings concerning program goal achievement and optimal Job Bank configuration were reported back to Manpower Administration officials in a series of papers and meetings, beginning in March of 1971 and ending in June of 1972.

Both administrators and academics have pointed out the difficulty of getting program operators to incorporate assessment results into manpower program structure and operation. Stanley Ruttenberg, former assistant secretary of labor for manpower, is pessimistic about the record in this regard. In 1970 Ruttenberg observed the following:

Unfortunately, government institutions have developed an almost impregnable screen against criticism. The usual reaction to criticism, whether constructive or not, is a flood of propaganda, conceding some validity to the criticism and admitting some room for improvement, but assuring the public that the situation is well in hand and that progress is the institution's most important product. Words become the accepted method of response Actions need not follow. A glance through the Annual Manpower Reports of the President since 1965 confirms that the employment service is no exception to this practice.[7]

Cain and Hollister, academics who have been actively involved in efforts to assess manpower programs, have attempted to explain the failure to use assessment results.

A major reason for this, we feel, is an inadequate taste for rigor (or an overweening penchant for visceral judgments) by administrators and legislators and excessive taste for the purely scientific standards by academics. It often seems that scholars conspire with the legislators to beat down any attempt to bring to bear more orderly evidence about the effectiveness of alternative programs; it is not at all difficult to find experts who will testify that virtually any evaluation study is not adequately "scientific" to provide a sound basis for making program decisions. There is a reasonable and appropriate fear on the part of academics that sophisticated techniques of analysis will be used as deceptive wrapping around an essentially political kernel to mislead administrators or the public. This fear, however, often leads to the setting of standards of "proof" which cannot, at present, given the state of the art of social sciences, or perhaps never, given the inherent nature of social action programs, be satisfied. The result generally is that the evaluation is discredited, the information it provides ignored, and the decision-maker and legislator can resume the exercise of their visceral talents.[8]

It was our intent to determine if, under relatively favorable conditions and with a rather intense program of feedback, we could in fact have an impact on the direction and structure of a manpower program. This was the third purpose of the research. If it could be shown that the results did effect decisions concerning the Job Bank Program, both administrators and academics might be encouraged to adopt a more positive view of human resource-manpower program analysis generally. Specifically, administrators might be helped to see the usefulness of moderately rigorous performance analysis, and academics might gain additional insights into the limitations of such analyses for decision-making.

Conclusions

Several conclusions were reached concerning each area of the research.

Achievement of Job Bank Goals

Present local Job Banks are not achieving four of the five goals on which we focused. Specifically, present local Job Banks are *not*:

1. Achieving more efficient man-job matching
2. Improving manpower service to the disadvantaged

3. Reducing frictional unemployment
4. Maintaining or increasing ES volume on overall activity measures

The final goal examined was: 5. Providing more flexible, more rapid, and more direct manpower services to employers and workers. It is clear that local Job Banks are not providing more rapid service. However, we could not satisfactorily define "flexibility," and we could obtain no data on "directness." Hence, we could draw no conclusions concerning achievement of this fifth goal.

Optimal Organizational Characteristics

Even though present local Job Banks are not achieving program goals, universal adoption of certain organizational attributes would lead to more nearly meeting all of the goals. Specifically, we concluded that Job Banks should be organized in the following way.

1. Both order-taking and referral units should be organized in a specialized fashion.
2. Agencies should be encouraged to maintain an adequate employer relations effort.
3. The Employment Service should minimize the involvement of community agencies in Job Banks.
4. Each interviewer should have his or her own Job Bank book or video display device.
5. First-day referral should be provided to the greatest possible extent.
6. State agencies should be encouraged to operate a relatively large number of local offices within each area, rather than concentrating operations in fewer offices.
7. Procedures for verifying referrals should be reexamined, as present telephone verification systems are not working well.

Effect of Feedback on the Program

The effect of feedback on the direction and structure of the program is clearly a result of its effect on the program administrators. We found it convenient to categorize our conclusions concerning feedback into those concerning its effect on administrators and those concerning its effect on the program. The conclusions concerning the administrators are the following.

1. The administrators of the program desired, sought, and sometimes acted upon recommendations for improving Job Banks.

2. The higher administrators in the Manpower Administration were consciously predisposed to be relatively insensitive, with respect to action-
taking, to feedback concerning negative findings. We believe that this is a
consequence of the more general conclusion that the effect of feedback is
a function of whether it is relevant to an immediately forthcoming
decision.
3. The administrators were inclined to accept facts and implications associated with positive findings and not to accept those associated with
negative findings.
4. The administrators were inclined to communicate positive findings and not
to communicate negative findings.
5. Policy seemed to be a more important determinant of program-related
decisions than was information about the effectiveness of the program.

The conclusions concerning the effect on the program are the following.

1. The findings concerning overall goal achievement, which were almost
entirely negative, have not had any effect on the Job Bank Program.
2. The findings concerning Job Bank organization have had an effect on the
ES National Office position regarding optimal organization.

2

Job Banks and the Design of the Job Bank Study

Origin, Status, and Future of Job Banks

The Job Bank Program was explicitly charged by the secretary of labor with contributing to the solution of the three information-related problems alluded to in the previous chapter: first, to reduce frictional unemployment through faster matching of workers and jobs; second, to improve manpower services to the disadvantaged through providing better job information faster and more equitably than was done in the previous system; and third, to achieve more efficient man-job matching in Public Employment Service placement operations.[1]

Background

Legislative direction and authorization for increased attention to labor-market information were provided in the 1968 amendments to the Manpower Development and Training Act (MDTA), Title I, Section 106. These amendments require the secretary of labor to "develop a comprehensive system of labor market information," and specifically directed in Subsection (b) that the secretary "develop and establish a program for matching the qualifications of unemployed, underemployed, and low-income persons with employer requirements and job opportunities. . . . In the development of such a program, the Secretary shall make maximum possible use of electronic data processing and telecommunications systems for the storage, retrieval, and communication of job and worker information."

To finance specific labor-market information activities, including those noted above, the amendments stated that "not less than 2 per centum of the sums appropriated in any fiscal year to carry out Titles I, II, and III of this act (MDTA) shall be available only for carrying out the provisions of subsection (b) of this section."

President Nixon expressed strong interest in labor-market information during the 1968 election campaign, by asserting that "in our concern to create job opportunities and to train people, we have largely ignored the problem of communication about jobs."[2] Noting that if computers could be used for matching boys and girls for college dates, they could be used for matching job-seeking men with man-seeking jobs, Mr. Nixon then called for immediate creation of a National Computer Job Bank.

7

Shortly after his inauguration, President Nixon directed the secretary of labor to follow through on his campaign demand for a National Computer Job Bank. On March 18, 1969, the secretary responded with a memorandum to the president, conveying Department of Labor plans in this area. The memorandum outlined a two-phased approach to the development of a national computer-aided job-matching network. The first proposed phase (initially scheduled to be completed by June 30, 1970) was the deployment of installations based on the Baltimore Job Bank design in at least thirty-six of the largest labor-market areas in the nation, coupled with exportation of the more sophisticated Utah man-job matching system to at least three additional states. The second phase proposed in the memorandum was the installation of Utah-type man-job matching systems, linked into a nationwide system tied together by a rapid telecommunications design. The second phase was to be completed by June 30, 1975.

As the above discussion documents, computer-assisted man-job matching has had strong support, both in Congress and at the highest levels of the Nixon administration. These programs were also given high priority by the then assistant secretary of labor for manpower, Arnold Weber, who had initial responsibility for implementing the Department of Labor's program in this area. Weber gave strong support for such programs in an article published late in 1969: "Public manpower programs should give continuing emphasis to the development of institutions that will improve the overall operation of the labor market. . . . Such efforts will help minimize the need for short-term, client oriented programs that divert Congress and bedevil public administrators. . . . Resort to 'out reach,' 'job development' and the other costly paraphernalia of the Concentrated Employment Program might not have been required if more resources had been allocated to the improvement of labor market information systems through the Job Bank and computerized matching systems."[3]

The Baltimore Job Bank[4]

The Job Bank concept was developed by the Maryland Department of Employment Security early in 1968, and the Baltimore Job Bank became operational in May of that year. The Job Bank does not use the computer to match people with jobs or training slots. Rather, it uses the computer to record and store brief descriptions of all job openings known to the employment service in the area.

Each evening filled jobs are deleted, new openings received are added, and the updated list is printed out in the form of a Job Bank book, copied, and distributed early the following morning to all counselors and placement interviewers in the Employment Service and cooperating Community Agencies. To avoid referring more applicants for a job than are desired by the employer and to keep from sending applicants to recently filled jobs, a central telephone-order control unit is included in the Job Bank system.

As developed in Maryland, the Job Bank involved a fairly drastic reorganization of Employment Service placement operations. Previously, placement interviewers both received and filled orders and usually specialized in particular occupations or industries. Now, almost all job orders are taken by a central unit whose members do not specialize in any way or make referrals. Referrals are made by placement interviewers who also do not specialize and who do not take job orders. Further, the Maryland Employment Service did not previously share job openings with other employment-oriented nonprofit Community Agencies. Now, all Employment Service job orders are made available to these agencies by means of the Job Bank book.

A third change in Employment Service organization usually associated with implementation of a Job Bank is the stationing of more placement interviewers in disadvantaged neighborhoods. Out-stationing of interviewers is much more feasible now because the Job Bank book gives them up-to-date data on all jobs listed in the system, something that was not possible before.

Several advantages were claimed for the Baltimore Job Bank. Some of these, such as the potential for better management control associated with automatic data-processing systems, are indisputable. Others, such as an increase in job orders and in placement of disadvantaged persons, definitely occurred in Baltimore, but may or may not have been attributable primarily to the Job Bank. Still other claimed outcomes in the Baltimore Job Bank, such as "no significant loss in the volume of total placements except in professional and clerical placements," eventually turned out to have somewhat bent the facts.

The Job Bank Program: Local Job Banks

In order to implement the decision to install Job Banks in various cities and to conduct other work in the area of computer-aided man-job matching, the Department of Labor established the Division of Manpower Matching Systems (DMMS) in April 1969. The division was established as part of the Office of Systems Support, U.S. Training and Employment Service, in the Manpower Administration. The chief of the division had previously been special assistant to the director, U.S. Employment Service. The staff initially assigned included fifteen professionals (two of whom were never involved in DMMS work) and six clericals.

The DMMS staff was divided into two major sections; one section had responsibility for expediting the installation of Job Banks, and the other section was involved in the longer-range task of helping develop more sophisticated systems along the lines of the Utah man-job matching system.

As noted earlier, the Department of Labor planned initially to install Job Banks in thirty-six large labor-market areas by June 30, 1970. Implementation of this aspect of the division work proceeded rapidly, as DMMS gave high priority to meeting the thirty-six city goal.

In negotiating with the Department of Labor over the specific form for their Job Banks, the individual state employment security agencies proposed many variations on the Baltimore model. Some of these variations are mechanical—for example, publishing job orders on microfilm and using viewers rather than printing the orders in book form. Others are organizational—such as retaining some specialization of placement interviewers rather than using the every-man-a-generalist approach taken in Baltimore.

Generally, the Labor Department has encouraged local variations, although three conditions have been required, at least in the earlier group of Job Banks. First, order-taking and placement interviewing cannot be done by the same individual. The purpose of this rule is to prevent "pocketing" by the interviewer, that is, keeping a personal inventory of openings.

Second, all Job Banks must provide for participation of Community Agencies. This coordinates community efforts to develop jobs for the disadvantaged and relieves employers of making multiple contacts with agencies serving the same applicant population.

Third, each state agency must create a manpower data-processing system team in connection with its Job Bank. This is to assure that each agency will acquire the staff needed for subsequent development and implementation of a fully computerized matching system.

The attention given by DMMS to implementing local Job Banks, combined with high-level Department of Labor and state agency enthusiasm, led to rapid expansion of the number of operational Job Banks. A manual Job Bank opened in Hartford in March 1969.[5] St. Louis and Portland opened Job Banks in June 1969. These openings were followed in October by Seattle, Chicago, and Washington, D.C. (at which opening the secretary of labor announced an expansion of the June 30, 1970 goal to fifty-six Job Banks).

The Pittsburgh Job Bank opened in November, and San Diego opened in December. Hence, at the close of calendar year 1969, nine Job Banks were in operation. In addition, five Job Banks were funded but not operational, and proposals covering seven Job Banks were in the review or negotiation process.

Implementation of local Job Banks proceeded rapidly during the first half of calendar year 1970. By the end of March, there were thirteen operational Job Banks, twenty-eight additional cities had been funded but were not operational, and four proposals were being reviewed in DMMS.

In early April, the assistant secretary of labor decided to install Job Banks in as many additional cities outside the fifty-six city goal as possible, provided the new cities had an SMSA population of at least 250,000.

With a strong drive in June, the interim goal of fifty-six cities was nearly achieved. At June 30, forty-two Job Banks were operational and three more opened the first week in July.[6]

Table 2-1 lists the cities which had operational Job Banks on or before June 30, 1970.

Table 2-1
Job Banks Operational by June 30, 1970

City	Date Operational	State
	1968	
1. Baltimore	May	Maryland
	1969	
2. Hartford	March	Connecticut
3. St. Louis	June	Missouri
4. Portland	June	Oregon
5. Seattle	October	Washington
6. Chicago	October	Illinois
7. District of Columbia	October	District of Columbia
8. Pittsburgh	November	Pennsylvania
9. San Diego	December	California
	1970	
10. Atlanta	January	Georgia
11. Kansas City	February	Missouri
12. Minneapolis-St. Paul	March	Minnesota
13. Columbus	March	Ohio
14. Phoenix	April	Arizona
15. Philadelphia	April	
16. Memphis	April	Tennessee
17. Bridgeport	April	
18. Birmingham	May	Alabama
19. Syracuse	May	New York
20. Little Rock	May	Arkansas
21. San Antonio	May	Texas
22. Wichita	May	Kansas
23. Denver	June	Colorado
24. Buffalo	June	
25. Cincinnati	June	
26. Des Moines	June	Iowa
27. Wilmington[a]	June	Delaware
28. Charleston	June	West Virginia
29. Columbia	June	South Carolina
30. Tulsa[a]	June	Oklahoma
31. Oklahoma City	June	
32. New Haven[a]	June	
33. Cleveland	June	
34. Toledo[a]	June	
35. Dayton[a]	June	
36. Boston	June	Massachusetts

Table 2-1 (cont.)

City	Date Operational	State
	1968	
37. Tacoma	June	
38. Greensboro	June	North Carolina
39. Omaha	June	Nebraska
40. New York City	June	
41. Miami	June	Florida
42. Albuquerque	June	New Mexico

aNot among original fifty-six cities

Beyond Local Job Banks: The Phased
Implementation Progression

In the initial stage, all of the present Job Banks were urban and local in scope; and it is these local Job Banks that are the subject of the present research. However, local Job Banks are only the first stage of the Manpower Administration's plans for an eventual national computer-aided job-matching network. A brief discussion of these plans, documented under the title of Phased Implementation Progression (PIP) will help put the present research in perspective.[7]

Job Bank Expansion. From the base of Job Banks established by June 30, 1970, Manpower Administration plans called for installation of additional Job Banks in all cities having an SMSA population of at least 250,000 and at least two local offices. At this point, the Job Bank system would serve over 50 percent of the nation's labor force.

Intrastate "Economic District" Job Banks were the proposed next stage of expansion, to begin in the January-March quarter of 1971. These Job Banks were intended to cover the natural economic areas within each state, building outward from major SMSAs in each area.

Regional or Interstate Job Banks were viewed as a natural extension of the Economic District Job Banks. Finally, a linking of the interstate-regional systems was projected to lead to a linked nationwide system by January 1973.

Program Consolidation and Development. The PIP paper called for a phase of program consolidation and development to be undertaken in parallel with other aspects of computer-aided matching development. In this regard, it was urged that work proceed to develop improved applicant assessment, job assessment, and job development aids. The basic point here is that with computers available, these processes can be undertaken in more sophisticated ways than is the case in a manual operation.

Batch Mode Matching. In this phase (July 1971 to January 1974) the computer would be used to do the actual matching of men and jobs. Specifically, overnight matching of applications and openings would be used to supplement use of Job Bank books in daily operations.

On-line Matching. With on-line matching, the interviewer no longer has a physical file of jobs from which to work. Rather, the interviewer relies entirely on access to a computer often located in another city. The interviewer inputs his applicant's characteristics, and the computer provides a set of jobs matching those characteristics. "On-line" means that the computer can respond directly to specific inputs, in contrast to the batch system in which a set of inputs are analyzed over a longer time period. This stage was scheduled initially to extend from January 1974 to January 1975.

Optimum Matching. The final phase discussed in the PIP paper, initially scheduled for implementation during calendar year 1975, is optimum matching. This approach differs from those discussed earlier in that optimization is "total" rather than "sequential." In sequential optimization the job order file is searched on behalf of a particular applicant, in a search for the best job for *him.* Then the same thing is done for the next applicant. However, one job is now missing from the file, and is no longer available for the second applicant, even though it may have been an ideal match with his characteristics.

In "total optimization," all possible applicant-opening matches are considered in the computer, and matching is done according to some instruction to the computer to choose the set of matches that most benefits all applicants and/or openings, according to the particular decision rule given the computer.

The Phased Implementation Progression stays well within the bounds of existing computing and psychometric technology. It is an attempt to study and overcome the difference between what is technologically possible and what is economically and organizationally practical.[8] The Job Bank part of the Phased Implementation Progression appears to be proceeding more or less on schedule. For example, a number of Economic District, Statewide, and Interstate Job Banks are currently operational, and in May 1972 the Manpower Administration announced to all state agencies the content, use, and availability of the nationwide Job Bank Openings Summary.[9]

Work is also continuing on the more sophisticated systems being developed as successors to Job Banks, although there are many problems associated with this task.[10] Hence, present plans call for continued evaluation and development from one step to the next. These plans appear to represent a considered compromise between the most rapid possible implementation and a desire to install the most efficient systems.

Research Design

As noted in the previous chapter there were three purposes of the overall research effort. Each purpose demanded a separate research design. In this section we briefly discuss the design and implementation of the research necessary to (1) assess the extent to which the Job Banks achieved their goals, (2) determine the optimal Job Bank design configuration, and (3) determine the effect of feedback about the achievement and design on the direction and structure of the program. The design and methodology of the research are discussed in detail in Appendix 1.

Assessing the Extent of Goal Achievement

Determining the extent to which the Job Banks achieved the goals established for them was a four-step task. The first step was to determine what these goals were. The goals and the sources of our information concerning them were discussed earlier. In that discussion it was noted that the achievement of only the labor-market goals was to be assessed.

The second step was to identify the necessary data for measuring goal achievement. This required developing operational measures for each goal. An important constraint on these measures was that they not require the collection, at the local office level, of information that was not already being collected. Discussions with local office personnel and informed Manpower Administration officials quickly allowed us to obtain several operational measures for most goals. The exceptions to this are noted later in this report. The operational measures finally chosen are listed in Table 2-2.

The third step was to provide for obtaining, at the National Office, the data corresponding to each operational measure. It was intended that this data be provided on a monthly basis by all Job Banks, and that preimplementation data be provided by a large number of Job Banks so that pre- and postimplementation performance comparisons could be made for these cities. The obtaining of this data was accomplished by designing and implementing the Job Bank Operations Review (JBOR) system. This is a computer-based data collection system that records the activities of the Local Employment Service offices in great detail. General Administration Letter (GAL) 1353, and its subsequent modifications, which made JBOR mandatory are reproduced in Appendix 3. The process of developing and implementing JBOR is described in Appendix 1.

The fourth step was to analyze the data. The analysis compared the change in the performance measures in Job Bank cities before and after Job Bank implementation with changes in the same time period in these performance measures in a set of comparison cities and in the United States as a whole. If the

Table 2-2
Performance Measures

1. Proportionate change in referrals of disadvantaged applicants; G, B, T.[a]
2. Proportionate change in referrals of nondisadvantaged applicants; G, B, T.
3. Proportionate change in total referrals; G, B, T.
4. Proportionate change in placements of disadvantaged applicants; G, B, T.
5. Proportionate change in placements of nondisadvantaged applicants; G, B, T.
6. Proportionate change in total placements; G, B, T.
7. Proportionate change in placements (including those of a temporary nature): Table 1
8. Proportionate change in placements (excluding those of a temporary nature): Table VII
9. Change in ratio of referrals to placements for disadvantaged applicants; G, B, T.
10. Change in ratio of referrals to placements for nondisadvantaged applicants; G, B, T.
11. Change in ratio of referrals to placements for applicants; G, B, T.
12. Change in proportion of disadvantaged placements in good, bad, and total jobs.
13. Change in proportion of nondisadvantaged placements in good, bad, and total jobs.
14. Change in proportion of individuals placed who were disadvantaged; G, B, T.
15. Change in proportion of placements of disadvantaged applicants that were in "good" jobs.
16. Change in proportion of placements of nondisadvantaged applicants that were in "good" jobs.
17. Change in proportion of placements of total applicants that were in "good" jobs.
18. Change in proportion of placements of disadvantaged applicants that were in high-salary jobs.
19. Change in proportion of placements of nondisadvantaged applicants that were in high-salary jobs.
20. Change in proportion of placements of total applicants that were in high-salary jobs.
21. Change in ratio of disadvantaged placements (including those of a temporary nature) to disadvantaged applicants.
22. Change in ratio of nondisadvantaged placements (including those of a temporary nature) in nondisadvantaged applicants.
23. Change in ratio of total placements (including those of a temporary nature) to total applicants.
24. Change in ratio of placements to openings received: Tables I and II.
25. Change in ratio of placements to openings received: Table VII.
26. Change in ratio of placements (including those of a temporary nature) to openings received (including those of a temporary nature).
27. Proportionate change in openings received (first data source); G, B, T.
28. Proportionate change in openings received (including those of a temporary nature).
29. Proportionate change in openings received for "good" jobs.
30. Proportionate change in mean time to fill openings; G, B, T.
31. Proportionate change in individual placements; G, B, T.
32. Proportionate change in new applications.

[a]G, B, and T stand for good, bad, and total. See Appendix B.

average Job Bank performance was superior to the average comparison city performance by a margin viewed as of practical significance, and was statistically significant, then it was tentatively concluded that local Job Banks achieved the goal to which the performance measure related. If such were the case for several of the measures related to a particular goal, then we concluded that the goal had been achieved.

Obtaining and maintaining adequate comparison cities was quite an arduous and to some extent unsuccessful task; it is described in Appendix 1. Details of the experimental design and the statistical procedures by which we "corrected" for the noncomparability of the Job Bank cities with the comparison cities are also described in Appendix 1.

Determining Optimal Job Bank Design

We undertook the task of determining the optimum organization design because it seemed to us that a "pass-fail" analysis of Job Banks would be insufficient. For a variety of reasons, in the area of public policy it is frequently reasonable to make marginal improvements in existing programs rather than to discontinue them and leave some goal still unfulfilled. The question, of course, is "exactly what are the improvements?"

Determining optimal organization design is a problem that has been explored by practitioners and behavioral scientists for a long time. The resulting principles or theories are frequently contradictory or in need of qualification based on the organization's environment, traditions, or personnel. In order to overcome these problems, it appeared to us that a rigorous empirical approach would be useful in those situations where it was possible. We found that it was possible to use this approach for determining optimum "levels" of the design variables of the Job Banks.

The approach involved three steps. The first step was to identify the key design variables. We accomplished this through discussions with knowledgeable people in the Department of Labor and by designing and conducting an interview study in the four SMSAs where Job Banks had been in operation the longest. The study involved semistructured interviews with Job Bank managers, Employment Service interviewers, and local employers.

The second step was to obtain information on the levels of these variables as they existed in the various Job Banks. There was in fact considerable variation among the Job Banks in the design profile that they manifested. We obtained this information with a questionnaire, completed for each Job Bank by a person familiar with its design and operation. The completion of this questionnaire was voluntary, and many cities went unreported. The effect of the consequent reduction on our data base is noted in Appendix 1.

The third step was determining the effect of these variables on the performance measures of Table 2-2. Only the particular design variables that seemed most critical and subject to change, if they were found to be at a less effective level, were included in our analysis. These key design variables are shown in Table 2-3. The particular levels of these variables that were correlated with the highest performance were to be identified as optimal levels and recommended for universal adoption among the Job Banks, unless there was some interactive effect with other variables that would preclude such adoption. The details of the statistical analysis used in determining the optimal design are described in Appendix 1.

Assessing the Impact of Feedback

This aspect of the research required a two-step procedure, with the two steps being conducted concurrently. One step was to develop and maintain a record of all decisions pertaining to the Job Bank Program, together with a listing of the reasons for the decision insofar as we could determine these. This was achieved

Table 2-3
Job Bank Variables

1. Job order-taking, specialized versus nonspecialized.
2. Applicant interviewing and referring, specialized versus nonspecialized.
3. Job opening inventory displays, hard copy versus CRT screen.
4. Number of community agencies, three or more versus two or less.
5. Ratio of job opening inventory display devices to interviewers, nonshared versus shared.
6. Ratio of full-time equivalent people working in multiservice centers to the number of full-time equivalent people working in placement-related activities.
7. Ratio of full-time equivalent people working in ES offices in poverty areas to the number of full-time equivalent people working in placement-related activities.
8. Ratio of full-time equivalent people who work as Employer Relations Representatives to the number of full-time equivalent people working in placement-related activities: Investigated as a continuous and dichotomous variable.
9. Number of conventional local offices having Job Bank books or viewers.
10. Proportion of openings filled the same day.
11. Proportionate change in the proportion of openings filled the same day.
12. Number of ES full-time equivalent persons involved in placement-related activities.
13. Number of ES full-time equivalent persons working as Employer Relations Representatives.
14. Proportion of verification by referring interviewer using mail, phone, or other means.
15. Proportion of referrals verified by phone.
16. Proportion of referrals verified by means other than phone.
17. Ratio of total walk-in transaction referrals to total transaction referrals.
18. Ratio of total walk-in transaction placements to total transaction placements.

by examining USTES files, reports, and other documents pertaining to the program, and by periodic discussion with USTES officials.

The second step was to periodically provide analyses of data bearing on Job Bank performance and optimal design to USTES officials. Through later discussions with these officials an effort was made to learn of any specific use made of these data in decision-making. A more complete description of these endeavors is contained in Appendix 1.

Findings Concerning the Performance and Design of Local Job Banks

Introduction

This report combines all of our findings and recommendations concerning the operation of local Job Banks. It includes new material, as well as data and results from similarly titled papers presented at meetings with USES officials in March, November, and December 1971, and March 1972.[1]

The major purpose of the paper is to pull together our recommendations for improving local Job Banks through promoting universal adoption of certain organizational attributes not presently used in every Job Bank city. The recommendations are based on our analysis of Job Bank Operations Review (JBOR) data from eighteen cities, and on three additional studies conducted earlier by us or under our supervision.[2]

A secondary purpose of the paper is to set forth our findings concerning the extent to which local Job Banks appear to be achieving the Public Policy or labor-market-related goals originally set for the Job Bank Program. Because our findings do not relate to all of the program's goals, and because we do not know what weight to assign the various goals, we do not attempt to make judgments concerning the overall success of local Job Banks.

Three important caveats should be kept in mind by the reader. First, all studies of the Job Banks to date, including this one, have necessarily concerned local Job Banks, i.e., SMSA-wide Job Banks. Local Job Banks are only a first step in the Phased Implementation Plan (PIP)[3] that will lead to a more-automated, nationwide manpower matching system. Thus our conclusions concerning the extent to which certain of the Job Bank program goals have been met apply only to this early, local Job Bank phase of the overall program. When and if studies are made of the later phases, the conclusions concerning the extent to which later phases of the program meet the goals may be different from those applying to this early phase.

We hasten to note that this caution concerning extrapolation of conclusions

---

This chapter was originally issued as the final and cumulative report of the researchers concerning the goal achievement and optimal design configuration of local Job Banks (USES Report). Only two notes have been added. The report was mailed to various U.S. Employment Service officials responsible for operating the Job Bank Program, including the director of USES, during the third week of June 1972; it was discussed with these same officials on June 26, 1972.

The appendixes to the USES report, which included the results of our statistical analysis, are included as Appendix 2.

does not apply to the recommendations regarding universal adoption of various organizational attributes. These organizational recommendations are applicable not only to local Job Banks, but also to the more advanced phases of the planned system.

The second caveat concerns the nonoptimal nature of the Job Banks studied. We found that considerably less than half of these Job Banks manifested the majority of the organizational attributes that we found to be optimal. If all of the Job Banks had manifested all of the optimal attributes, our conclusions concerning the extent to which certain of the program goals were met may have been more favorable.

The third caveat concerns the timing of the JBOR data. Data covering thirty performance measures, twelve organizational attributes, and three control variables were used in the study. Data for February and March 1970 (pre-Job Bank) were compared with analogous data for February and March 1971 (post-Job Bank). Unfortunately, unemployment rose in study cities an average of 1.3 percentage points between the 1970 and 1971 periods. Because of this change in labor-market environment and despite our efforts to control for this change, our conclusions may be limited to, or affected by, such a change in labor market.

We note here that we have carefully examined the effect of unemployment rate change on each of our variables, and we believe our recommendations and conclusions would be applicable even if the unemployment rate had been stable. We are especially confident in this regard concerning our organizational recommendations, because some of the earlier studies leading to the same recommendations were conducted under more stable labor-market conditions. We turn now to an enumeration and discussion of our organizational recommendations.

Recommendations[4]

1. Both order-taking and referral units should be organized in a specialized fashion. All data analyzed confirm what employer interview studies have consistently concluded: specialization of order-takers and referral interviewers leads to better man-job matches.[5] More importantly, the JBOR data analysis also showed that service to the disadvantaged is not better in Job Banks organized along nonspecialized lines than elsewhere. Hence, all groups of clients gain from specialization of order-taking and referral units.

2. Agencies should be encouraged to maintain an adequate employer relations effort. The data examined here confirm the need for such efforts. Cities placing relatively heavy emphasis on employer relations work attracted significantly more and better openings than did cities with less employer relations emphasis. These relationships held throughout the range of our data; that is, no city in our sample placed so much emphasis on employer relations that key variables, such as proportion of regular placements in "good DOT"

jobs, proportion of regular placements in jobs paying at least $2.50 per hour, and proportion of applicants placed, were adversely affected.

3. The Employment Service should minimize the involvement of other agencies in Job Banks. Service to employers and to both disadvantaged and other applicants was revealed by our analysis to be poorer in those Job Banks most strongly emphasizing Community Agency (CA) involvement. Given the relatively small role played by CAs in nearly all Job Banks, it appears that little would be lost by minimizing their involvement. This proposal must be tempered to the extent that CA involvement is desirable for reasons unrelated to Job Bank goals. If it is determined that CA involvement in Job Banks is necessary, high priority should be given to training CA personnel in placement fundamentals.

4. Each interviewer should have his or her own Job Bank book or video display device. The data showed that interviewer access to listings is a prerequisite to adequate service to applicants and employers. Service measures were better where interviewers had better access to a Job Bank book or video display device.

5. First-day referral should be provided to the greatest possible extent. JBOR data show that local Job Banks have not reduced overall time to fill openings, despite the broader exposure to openings inherent in the system. Failure to routinely provide first-day service in some Job Banks is the reason for the lack of reduction in time to fill openings.

6. Agencies should be encouraged to operate a relatively large number of local offices within each area, rather than concentrating operations in fewer offices. JBOR data show that number of local offices is positively associated with a decline in time to fill openings and with a higher ratio of placements to openings received.

7. Procedures for verifying referrals should be reexamined as present telephone verification systems are not working well. Central telephone verification, typical of many Job Banks, appears to result in poorer matches, thus causing a decline in placements and job orders. Emphasis on interviewer verfication improves aspects of service to employers, but works against the interests of disadvantaged applicants.

8. Job Bank Operations Review data, or other performance data, should be collected and analyzed to determine the effect of the organizational changes recommended here. Although the universal adoption of the organizational changes proposed here will, in our judgment, move Job Banks toward better performance, the actuality and extent of these improvements should be confirmed after they are implemented.

Findings Underlying the Recommendations

Order-taking and Referral Unit Organization. The JBOR data analysis reveals only one difference in performance between those Job Banks in which order-taking is specialized and those in which order-taking is not specialized: year-to-year changes in referral/placement ratios increased in cities with non-specialized order-taking. Given that there were no changes in other variables, the greater increase in referral/placement ratios clearly suggest poorer service to employers and applicants and is undesirable.

This finding confirms the results of employer interview studies, which indicate that employers in cities in which Job Bank order-taking was not specialized often complained that referred applicants did not meet the specifications on their orders.

Findings concerning referral units parallel the above. Referral/placement ratios were up more in cities with nonspecialized referral units, especially for high and medium-skill jobs which require more knowledgeable interviewers. Placements were also down significantly more in cities with nonspecialized referral units.

Although there were only two cities with nonspecialized referral units, we accept the statistical findings because the employer-interview studies so strongly confirm them. Employers in cities with nonspecialized referral units frequently remarked that referred applicants did not match their openings. Employers also complained about the lack of personal service associated with Job Banks with nonspecialized referral units. Clearly, high referral/placement ratios and de-clining placements are evidence of poor matching in the nonspecialized cities.

Agencies Should Be Encouraged to Maintain an Adequate Employer Relations Effort. JBOR data support the present emphasis on employer relations activities. The proportion of applicants placed, particularly nondisadvantaged applicants, is higher in cities where full-time equivalent employer relations representatives are a higher proportion of total staff. Thus the probability that a particular applicant will be placed is enhanced by devoting more staff to employer relations activities.

The quality of job openings received is also favorably affected by employer relations effort. The proportion of total placements that are in high or medium-skill jobs is higher in cities where full-time equivalent employer relations representatives are a higher proportion of total staff.

Where employer relations representatives constituted less than 10 percent of all placement-related staff, an average of 4 percent of regular placements were in jobs paying at least $2.50 per hour. On the other hand, in cities where the ratio of employer relations representatives to total placement-related staff was 10 percent or more, 11 percent of regular placements were in jobs paying $2.50 per hour or more. Extrapolating this result to national data would have led to an increase in the number of $2.50-and-over jobs in calendar year 1970, from 106,000 to 291,000.

The Employment Service Should Minimize the Involvement of Other Agencies in Job Banks. Analysis of JBOR data reveals that both referrals and placements declined significantly more in cities with three or more Community Agencies (CAs) associated with the Job Bank than elsewhere. Inclusion of several CAs appears to have an especially adverse effect on placements in better jobs: both the proportion of placements in jobs paying $2.50 per hour or more, and the proportion of placements in high and medium-skill jobs, declined most in cities with three or more associated CAs.

Disadvantaged applicants appear to be most affected by including CAs. The disadvantaged proportion of total placements declined most where there were three or more CAs associated with Job Bank.

All of our earlier studies of Job Bank support the conclusion that CA involvement has a negative effect on service to employers and applicants. Employers interviewed in these studies were much less critical of Job Banks in cities with less CA involvement than where there was more CA involvement. The gist of the complaint was that referral quality dropped where there was heavy CA involvement.

The JBOR data suggest that employer concern over CA involvement leads to a falloff in order quality and to less willingness to consider disadvantaged applicants. Thus service, to the very group CAs are set up to help, actually deteriorates when CAs are heavily involved in Job Banks.

Each Interviewer Should Have His of Her Own Job Bank Book or Video Display Device. The JBOR data show that placements declined more and referral/placement ratios increased more in cities with fewer books or video display devices than elsewhere. The increase in referral/placement ratios was most pronounced for high and medium-skill jobs.

First-Day Referral Should Be Provided to the Greatest Possible Extent. First, average time to fill openings was closely related to emphasis on first-day referral: time to fill openings was less where first-day placements increased. Also, placements and openings fell less where the proportion of openings filled on the first day rose after Job Bank. Finally, placements fell less in cities in which a high proportion of openings were filled on the first day.

Agencies Should Be Encouraged to Operate a Relatively Large Number of Local Offices within Each Area, Rather than Concentrating Operations in Fewer Offices. Time to fill openings declined more in cities with a larger number of offices. This finding is consonant with our expectations: the more widely openings are shared, i.e., the more contacts within the local labor market, the greater the impact Job Bank should have on time to fill openings. Further, filling openings faster should lead to filling a higher percentage of openings received, because timeliness is the essence of placement.

Procedures for Verifying Referrals Should Be Reexamined, Because Present Telephone Verification Systems Are Not Working Well. Central telephone verification was strongly and positively associated with rising referral/placement ratios, falling placements, and declining job orders. These results suggest that poorer matches are being achieved in Job Banks emphasizing central telephone verification. On the other hand, in cities where a high proportion of referral verification was conducted by interviewers, nondisadvantaged and total placements fell less, referral of nondisadvantaged and total applicants to "bad" DOT jobs rose more, and the disadvantaged proportion of placements rose less than in other cities. Taken together, these findings suggest that interviewer verification is a manifestation of an employer-oriented approach. The outcome described would be highly satisfactory to most employers, but not to other client groups, particularly disadvantaged applicants.

No recommendations are being made concerning five other organizational attributes of local Job Banks, because our findings are not conclusive or do not suggest the superiority of particular organizational forms. These attributes are the following.

1. Ratio of full-time equivalent staff in multiservice centers to full-time equivalent placement staff.
2. Ratio of full-time equivalent staff stationed in poverty areas to full-time equivalent placement personnel.
3. Output form: hard copy vs. video display devices.
4. Number of Employment Service placement personnel.
5. Ratio of walk-in referrals to total referrals.

**Estimating the Impact of the
Proposed Changes**

At the December 1971 meeting with Manpower Administration officials, the following question was raised: how much improvement in performance measures would have resulted from universal adoption of the proposed design attribute forms? For the reasons given below, we subsequently concluded that our present data should not be used to answer this question.

No Job Bank city in our sample has more than four of the six proposed design attributes, and only four of the eighteen Job Banks have as many as four attributes.[6] As will be clear from the following discussion, this fact prevents us from confidently estimating the magnitudes of the differences our proposed design would make in Job Bank performance, even though the analysis reinforces our belief that our proposed design would lead to superior performance.

We had March 1970 and March 1971 data for three of the four "best-designed"—i.e., four attributes included—Job Banks in our sample. We compared the year-to-year change in placements in these three cities with the comparable figure for our twelve comparison cities. The mean decline in placements in the comparison cities was 24.7 percent. Placements in the three best-designed Job Banks declined 21.4 percent, 11.1 percent and 6.0 percent, for an average decline of 12.8 percent. Although there is an impressive difference between the average change in Job Bank and comparison cities, and all three Job Banks did better than did the average comparison city, there is too much variation in results for the three Job Banks for one to put much faith in the average change. Presumably, our three best-designed Job Banks would have done even better, by an indeterminant amount, if they had had all six of the proposed attributes.[7]

Findings Concerning Program Goals

We have inferred nine Job Bank Program goals from Department of Labor (DOL) documents and from discussions with Manpower Administration officials. The main source document used in determining program goals was a March 18, 1969 memorandum from Secretary of Labor Shultz to President Nixon, conveying the DOL plans for creating a National Computer Job Bank.

Five goals pertain directly to the role of the Public Employment Service in the labor market. These goals are: (1) achieve more efficient matching; (2) improve manpower service to the disadvantaged; (3) reduce frictional unemployment; (4) provide more flexible, rapid, and direct manpower services to employers and workers; and (5) maintain or increase Employment Service volume on overall activity measures.

The remaining four goals concern internal aspects of Employment Service operation, are primarily of interest to agency management, and do not have significant direct implications for labor-market functioning. These goals are: (1) achieve more effective management controls; (2) improve the public image of the Employment Service; (3) improve the morale of Employment Service personnel; and (4) accomplish all program objectives with no increase in the direct cost of manpower services.

Our analysis has focused almost entirely on the five labor-market, or public policy, goals for two reasons. First, our primary interest in Job Banks is as an instrument of public policy: How can Job Banks improve labor-market functioning? JBOR was designed with this question in mind, and thus the JBOR data bear primarily on the five labor-market goals.

The second reason we have emphasized labor-market goals, rather than internal operations or management goals, is that other studies appear to have examined the latter goals more closely. In particular, the Ultrasystems study developed data pertaining to internal operations goals that appear superior to our data bearing on these issues.[8]

Even though we limit our conclusions to the five labor-market-related goals, it appears worthwhile to share our findings. The format for the discussion will be the following. First, the individual goal will be listed, together with our a priori expectation concerning the result of the tests. Second, the test(s) of goal achievement will be listed. Third, the present evidence pertaining to degree of goal achievement will be set forth, and finally a conclusion will be given. In general, we measured the goal achievement of Job Banks by comparing, for the Job Bank cities, pre-Job Bank performance data with post-Job Bank performance data; and then we compared the resulting differences with the difference that occurred in a set of non-Job Bank comparison cities,[9] and with data for the United States as a whole.

Goal 1: Achieve More Efficient Man-Job Matching

Job Banks improve only the extensiveness of job-market information, i.e., the number of job openings made available to a particular applicant. Although this increase in extensiveness was a major factor in the decision to expand the Job Bank concept, the usefulness and impact of the increased extensiveness is open to some argument.

One argument which suggests that the increase is limited in its usefulness is that in the non-Job Bank employment service operation all job-market information of a particular kind is usually handled within one office. For example, all accountant applications and openings are routed through the Professional and Commercial Office. A local Job Bank is unlikely to improve significantly the number or exposure of accountant listings, because the type of openings or workers known to offices other than the Professional Office are unlikely to be of interest to accountants or their employers.

Another argument suggests that increases in the number and exposure of openings are of limited use at the lower end of the occupational spectrum. In a loose job market, an employer with openings in relatively unskilled occupations usually can fill them by having them exposed through a single Employment Service office, so listing in a Job Bank book may not be particularly advantageous. Conversely, in a very tight job market, an applicant searching for a relatively unskilled job may not need any more information than that which is available in a single local office. Finally, in markets in which the Employment Service does not have good penetration, the total number of openings available to applicants may not be very large, regardless of how widely the listings are disseminated.

Job Banks do not directly affect the intensiveness of information, i.e., the amount of detail, included in the system.[10] Information contained in Job Bank descriptions of openings is essentially the same as the information on a conventional job order in a pre-Job Bank system. In practice, however, workers and placement interviewers in many Job Banks now get less detailed job information than they do under the alternative arrangement in which interviewers both take job orders and make referrals in particular occupations or industries. The order-taker/placement interviewer who specializes often has detailed information about the requirements of a job or employer that is not contained on the job order. In addition, the separation of order-taking and referral may result in some loss of information, in that some employer preference may not get written down or communicated from the order taken to the referral interviewers.

Rees and others have pointed out that the intensive aspects of information are the most crucial in labor markets.[11] Despite this argument, it appears likely that Job Banks improve the job-market information available to most Employment Service applicants, especially those without highly specific skills. For the least skilled, the loss of intensive information associated with most Job Banks is not of great importance when weighed against the large improvement in extensive information. However, for the skilled worker, and in many cases, for the employer, a local Job Bank offers little or no improvement in job-market information. To the extent that intensiveness is lost, the information may actually be less good than in the previous system from the skilled worker's or employer's point of view.

As a consequence of the above reasoning, our a priori expection was that local Job Banks would not lead to more efficient man-job matching.

Tests. Compare the following data for comparable months pre- and post-Job Banks, with corresponding data for non-Job Bank SMSAs and the United States.

1. Ratio of referrals to placements
2. Number of referrals
3. Ratio of persons placed to applicants
4. Ratio of placements to openings received
5. Number of placements
6. Time required to fill openings

Results. Data on the above variables were collected for Job Bank cities, several non-Job Bank (comparison) cities, and for the United States as a whole. All statistically significant differences among Job Bank cities and other areas are spelled out below.

1. Ratio of referrals to placements. Changes were similar in Job Bank and comparison cities; U.S. data were not available. Job Banks do not appear to have affected referral-placement ratios overall.
2. Number of referrals. Referrals declined slightly less in Job Banks than in comparison cities in March but not in February. U.S. data were not available. Job Banks may tend to increase the level of referrals.

3. Ratio of persons placed to applicants. Declines in Job Bank cities were significantly greater than in the United States as a whole, but were not different from comparison cities. Job Banks probably do not affect the ratio of persons placed to applicants.
4. Ratio of placements to openings received. Declined more in Job Bank cities than in the United States, but change was not different in Job Bank and comparison cities. Job Banks probably do not affect the ratio of placements to openings received.
5. Number of placements. Changes in regular placements were similar in Job Bank cities, comparison cities, and the United States as a whole. Job Banks do not appear to have affected regular placements.
6. Time to fill openings. As will be discussed at length in a later section, Job Banks do not appear to have reduced average time to fill job openings.

Conclusion. Considering all of the above results, it does not appear that local Job Banks have led to more efficient man-job matching.

*Goal 2: Improve Manpower Service
to the Disadvantaged*

There are two major reasons to expect the Job Bank Program to be especially beneficial to disadvantaged applicants. First, availability of openings to all interviewers should reduce the practice of "playing favorites," and this should benefit the disadvantaged because they are unlikely to be the "favorites" of interviewers.

A second reason for expecting Job Bank to benefit disadvantaged applicants is that, in most Job Bank cities, job openings are more available to disadvantaged applicants than is the case in non-Job Bank cities. For example, the Community Agencies involved in Job Bank serve disadvantaged applicants primarily. Previously, these agencies did not usually have access to Employment Service job openings. In addition, in many cities storefront offices were opened in poverty areas in connection with the installation of the Job Bank, thus making Employment Service openings more available to disadvantaged workers.

There is one reason to expect that Job Bank will adversely effect the placement opportunities of disadvantaged applicants. To the extent that disadvantaged workers will benefit from knowing about more and better jobs, Job Bank should indeed help them. However, it is unclear whether or not widespread dissemination of job information will necessarily alter the allocation of jobs to the benefit of the disadvantaged. In loose labor markets, widespread availability of job openings information may *hurt* the chances of the applicant less able to compete: if the more qualified workers also know about a job, the disadvantaged worker is unlikely to be hired.

Because of our inability to weight the conflicting forces discussed above, we had no priori expectations concerning the overall effect of local Job Banks on service to the disadvantaged.

Tests. Compare the following items for comparable months pre- and post-Job Bank, with corresponding data for non-Job Bank SMSAs and the United States.

1. Number of disadvantaged placements
2. Number of disadvantaged persons placed
3. Ratio of disadvantaged referrals to disadvantaged placements
4. Ratio of disadvantaged placements to disadvantaged new applicants
5. Time required to fill openings
6. Wages of disadvantaged placements
7. DICTIONARY OF OCCUPATIONAL TITLES occupation code of disadvantaged placements

Results. The significant differences among Job Bank cities and other areas revealed by our analysis are set forth below.

1. Number of disadvantaged placements. The number of regular placements of disadvantaged applicants is not significantly different in Job Bank cities than elsewhere. Further, Job Banks do not appear to have affected disadvantaged applicants differently from nondisadvantaged applicants as measured by number of placements.
2. Number of disadvantaged persons placed has not been significantly affected by local Job Banks.
3. Ratio of disadvantaged referrals to disadvantaged placements. The changes in referral/placement ratio were not significantly different for disadvantaged applicants than for other applicants.
4. Ratio of disadvantaged placements to disadvantaged new applicants. The probability that a disadvantaged applicant would be placed was significantly better in Job Bank cities than in the United States as a whole. However, there was not a significant difference in this regard between Job Bank cities and comparison cities.
5. Time required to fill openings. As local Job Banks do not appear to have speeded the filling of openings, applicants are not being placed more quickly. Hence, this aspect of service to the disadvantaged has not improved.
6. Wages of disadvantaged applicants. Although the change in proportion of disadvantaged placement in March in $2.50-and-over jobs rose significantly, the proportion of nondisadvantaged placements in such jobs rose by a similar amount. Further, in February the year-to-year change in proportion of disadvantaged placements in jobs paying $2.50 or more was

not significant. Hence, local Job Banks do not appear to have improved this aspect of service to the disadvantaged.

7. DICTIONARY OF OCCUPATIONAL TITLES occupation code of disadvantaged placements. The changes in high and medium-skill jobs were not statistically significantly different between the pre- and postperiods. It should be pointed out that failure to increase the disadvantaged share of better jobs is independent of the change in unemployment rate. Disadvantaged persons fared no better in this regard in cities where unemployment rose only slightly than in cities with a large increase in the unemployment rate.

Conclusion. Local Job Banks may have improved the probability that a disadvantaged applicant will be placed. However, other measures do not indicate improvement in service to this clientele. Of particular consequence is the indication that Job Banks have not improved access to better jobs for the disadvantaged. On balance, the data analyzed here do not support the view that Job Banks have been successful in improving service to the disadvantaged.

Goal 3: Reduce Frictional Unemployment

Conceptually, it is reasonable to expect Job Banks to result in faster placing of workers, because applicants are exposed to many more openings and this raises the probability of a "hit." If workers are placed faster, frictional unemployment will be reduced, because most Employment Service applicants are unemployed.[12] On the other hand, there is likely to be variation in the impact of Job Banks in this regard, because of differences among cities in the way orders are handled on the day of receipt. In some cities, unless the employer insists on "first-day referral," no interviewer is allowed to refer an order until it becomes available to all interviewers, the day *after* it is received. Where this practice prevails, virtually no openings are filled the day they are received. If, in the pre-Job Bank operation, say 10 or 20 percent of the openings were filled the day they were received, Job Bank could actually slow the filling of openings and increase frictional unemployment. In any event, where fewer openings are filled on the first day than was formerly the case, the Job Bank will have to be very effective to more than offset this handicap and thus speed *average* time to fill openings.

Test. Compare "Number of Calendar Days Required to Fill Job Openings" for comparable months pre- and post-Job Bank. ("Data on number of calendar days required to obtain a job," which would permit a direct measure of change in frictional unemployment due to Job Banks, is not available. Hence, the openings measure is used in the belief that it indirectly measures frictional unemployment: the only way in which workers can be placed more rapidly is for openings to be filled more quickly; and if openings are filled more quickly, workers must be getting placed more rapidly.)

Results. In the cities studied, there was an average decrease in time to fill openings of 2.5 days in February and 1.3 days in March. However, investigation shows that this decline was due to the rise in unemployment that occurred between the 1970 and 1971 months. In cities with a larger than average year-to-year rise in the unemployment rate, time to fill openings declined considerably. On the other hand, in cities with a small increase in unemployment rate, time to fill openings declined only slightly or not at all.

At one meeting with USES officials at which some of these findings were discussed, it was suggested that shifts in the occupational mix of the jobs being processed in Job Banks might affect the average time to fill openings. We have examined the relationships between time to fill openings and occupational mix in order to be assured that such a change in mix was not affecting our results.

Four tests were made for each of the four months on which this study is focusing: We examined (1) mean time to fill "good DOT" jobs as a function of proportion of jobs in "good DOT" categories; (2) mean time to fill "bad DOT" jobs as a function of the proportion of jobs in "bad DOT" categories; (3) mean time to fill all jobs as a function of the proportion of jobs in "good DOT" categories; and (4) mean time to fill all jobs as a function of the proportion of jobs in "bad DOT" categories.

This analysis did not reveal a significant relationship between time to fill openings and occupational mix. Hence, we conclude that changes or lack of changes in time to fill openings should not be attributed to changes in the occupational composition of jobs being processed.[13]

Conclusion. By our measure, local Job Banks do not appear to have reduced the level of frictional unemployment.

*Goal 4: Provide More Flexible, More
Rapid, and More Direct Manpower Services to
Both Employers and Workers*

This goal statement is taken verbatim from the March 18, 1969 memo from the secretary of labor to the president, from which we inferred most Job Bank goals. In this instance, the precise meaning of the goal is unclear. In particular, the meaning of the words "flexible" and "direct" are uncertain in the context of a Job Bank.

Because we were not able to specify the operational meaning of flexibility, we did not attempt to develop relevant measures of goal achievement. Thus we cannot draw conclusions concerning this goal.[14]

We presume "directness" to refer to the number of steps or actions occurring in the process of matching workers and employers. If our presumption is correct, then the extent to which Job Banks provide "directness" is dependent on just how the particular Job Bank is organized. We did not examine Job Bank work flows in sufficient detail to permit a comprehensive judgment on this matter. Clearly, some devices such as open Job Bank books in a self-service situation *increase* the directness of service. On the other hand, separation of order-taking, referral and verification into separate units certainly *reduces* directness, in comparison with a situation in which the individual interviewer is the single link between the applicant and the employer.

"More rapid service" is easier to define. Clearly, service rapidity refers to the amount of time required to refer or place applicants and refer on or fill job orders. As discussed under Goal 3, our a priori expectation was that Job Banks would lead to more rapid referral, placement, and order-filling, except in situations where first-day referral was reduced from the pre-Job Bank level.

Test. Compare "Number of Calendar Days Required to fill Job Openings" for comparable months pre- and post-Job Bank.

Results. As noted earlier, Job Banks do not appear to have reduced the time required to fill openings.

Conclusion. Local Job Banks do not appear to have led to providing more rapid service to either applicants or employers. We cannot draw conclusions concerning the overall effect of local Job Banks on either the flexibility or directness of service to employers or applicants.

Goal 5: Maintain or Increase Volume
on Overall Activity Measures

Achievement of this goal depends on the Public Employment Service increasing its share of labor-market activity. Unlike Goals 1 through 4, achievement of this goal is not necessarily indicative of improved labor-market performance. Nevertheless, it is an important institutional goal, as shown by internal documents. Further, a significant increase in the market share of the Public Employment Service would be important from a public policy viewpoint. For example, discussions concerning new manpower programs or welfare reform proposals invariably cover the question of the ability of the Employment Service to secure a large share of labor-market transactions. For example, can the public employment service secure sufficient job openings to implement the administration's welfare reform proposals?

Examination of historical trends in Employment Service activity measures reveals them to be quite stable. For example, number of new applications received by the Employment Services in calendar year 1961 through calendar year 1970 ranged from 9.8 million to 10.9 million. Referrals varied from 10.8 to 13.7 million during the same decade. These changes seem small indeed, given the wide swings that occurred in this decade in the unemployment rate (annual average ranged from 3.5 percent to 6.7 percent), in Employment Service budgets ($108 million to $433 million), and in program emphases (e.g., increasing attention to disadvantaged applicants).

Because of the relative stability of Employment Service activity measures over time, we expected Job Banks to have little effect on overall activity measures.

Test. Compare the following items for comparable months pre- and post-Job Bank, with similar data for non-Job Bank areas. SMSAs and the United States.

1. Number of placements
2. Number of regular placements
3. Number of openings received
4. Number of new applications received

Results. Data on the above variables were collected for Job Bank cities, several non-Job Bank (comparison) cities, and for the United States as a whole. All statistically significant differences among Job Bank cities and other areas are spelled out below.

1. Number of placements. Placements appear to have declined more in Job Bank cities than in comparison cities or the United States as a whole.
2. Number of regular placements. The changes in regular placements were similar in Job Bank cities, comparison cities, and the United States as a whole. Local Job Banks do not appear to have affected regular placements.
3. Number of openings received. Changes in number of openings received were similar in Job Bank cities, comparison cities, and the United States as a whole. Local Job Banks do not appear to have affected number of openings received.
4. Number of new applications received. Changes in number of new applications received were similar in Job Bank cities, comparison cities, and the United States as a whole. Local Job Banks do not appear to have affected the number of new applications received.

Conclusion. It does not appear that local Job Banks have increased the volume of overall Employment Service activity measures. Placements may have been adversely affected by local Job Banks.

Conclusions

This paper has set forth our recommendations for universal adoption of certain organizational attributes in Job Banks and has presented findings concerning the extent to which local Job Banks have achieved some of the goals initially set for the Job Bank Program. Although our findings concerning achievement of goals are neutral to negative, our findings concerning the effect of organizational attributes suggest that universal adoption of the associated recommendations would lead to more nearly meeting these goals.

It should be reemphasized here that our findings are based on a study of only local Job Banks, and later phases of the program may more nearly meet the goals of the Job Bank Program. Indeed, it is possible to speculate in this regard concerning the next stage of the Phased Implementation Plan (PIP), that of multimarket Job Banks. It seems quite possible that time to fill openings will decline in occupations for which the market is more than local, when Job Banks are expanded beyond local boundaries. Similarly, several measures of man-job matching efficiency, e.g., referral/placement ratios, could conceivably improve in an expanded Job Bank. On the other hand, multimarket Job Banks are unlikely to lead to improved service to disadvantaged applicants. In general, placements of such applicants are in occupations for which the labor market is local; thus there is little potential for improved service to the disadvantaged in expanded Job Banks.

The present study casts no light on the probable performance of the more sophisticated computer-aided matching systems currently being developed in the Public Employment Service. Hence, these findings should not be interpreted to suggest either abandoning the Phased Implementation Plan or accelerating the movement to more sophisticated systems. Rather it is hoped that the findings will aid the Employment Service in its efforts to evolve the most effective possible computer-aided manpower matching system.

**Findings Concerning the
Effect of Feedback on
Program Administration
and Administrators**

This chapter has three parts. The first deals with the ethical problems associated with a case study such as ours. The second briefly discusses each of the principal decisions and decision-related-events concerning the Job Bank Program between its inception and June 1972. The various bodies of data pertaining to Job Bank performance and design are also spelled out. The discussion is in chronological order to facilitate examining and understanding the relationship between decision-making and performance assessment. .

The third section of the chapter is an interpretation of the events listed in the second section. This third section traces the relation between available performance data and decision-making, in an effort to weigh the extent to which available data affected decisions and to spell out the reasons that the data appear not always to have been fully utilized.

Ethical Problems

In reporting his detailed anthropological study of the operation of one department within a state employment agency, Peter Blau was able to maintain the anonymity of the people whose activities he studied.[1] This was because there are many state employment agencies and many departments within each. Unfortunately we are not able to maintain the anonymity of the people whose activities we observed. Our study, for a number of reasons, is well known in the Manpower Administration, the largest subunit within the U.S. Department of Labor. Descriptions of, and references to, this research have appeared in a number of Manpower Administration publications, including some initiated by the very officials whose activities we studied.

There are some undesirable consequences of this. For example we know, as did Weiss and Rein, that "the data can affect the social standings and careers of individuals, as well as the success of the strategies of interest groups."[2] Hence, we feel compelled to point out that these officials were involved in the initiation of, and fully supported, this research. It is our belief that their motives in this regard were altruistic and their behavior commendable. If this study is a contribution to the science and practice of administration, these administrators made it so.

We think that the content of the remainder of this chapter will show that we have not allowed our respect for the actions of these administrators in one area to interfere with our reporting of their actions in another. We are in agreement with, and believe that we have successfully followed, the thinking of Weiss and Rein.

Investigators are committed to report, after the conclusion of their study, all data which bear on evaluation of the program. This commitment limits the situations in which they can promise confidentiality. Yet even if they have not made this promise, they often feel constrained to do no damage to those who have cooperated with them. At times it may appear that investigators are more protective of members of the community than those members are of themselves; but the investigator must remain aware of the potential effect of his appraisals on individuals and groups. If there is no way an investigator can describe what happened without making clear that one individual blocked action, or another failed to carry through an agreement, then perhaps the best he can do is state the circumstances from all perspectives so that a reader can understand that the behaviors were plausible in the circumstances. . . .

If there is a sponsoring agency which requires information regarding the viability of its program, there can be no disguises of critical information without compromising the initial commitment of the investigator.[3]

While we did not manipulate the facts, we did attempt to depersonalize the report, and at the same time make it more understandable to readers unfamiliar with the Department of Labor organization. For example, the principal direct recipients of our feedback were three hierarchically-organized USTES administrators in charge of the Job Bank Program. We refer to them as the lower-level administrator (LLA), the middle-level administrator (MLA), and the upper-level administrator (ULA). Three other direct recipients were three hierarchically-organized OPER administrators whom we refer to as LLR-OPER, MLR-OPER, and ULR-OPER. Three potential recipients were three hierarchically organized DOL officials who played key roles in making top level policy decisions about the program. We refer to them by their titles, the secretary of labor, the assistant secretary of labor for manpower, and his deputy, the manpower administrator. The USTES and OPER administrators reported to these three officials.

Chronology of Job Bank Decisions
and Performance Data Availability

I. Decision: To develop a National computer-aided job-matching network.
    Formal date of decision: January 30, 1969
    Bases for decision: (a) The 1968 amendments to the Manpower Development and Training Act provided legislative authorization and direction for such a program; (b) President Nixon called for a National Computer Job Bank during the 1968 election campaign.
    Decision codified by: Directive from President Nixon to the secretary of

labor instructing the secretary to create a National Computer Job Bank System.

Empirical evidence available to decision-makers: None to our knowledge.

II. Decision: To install Job Banks based on the Baltimore design in at least thirty-six of the largest labor-market areas in the nation by June 30, 1970.

Formal date of decision: March 18, 1969

Bases for decision: (a) Priority needs of large cities; (b) need for immediate implementation of most economical and efficient system available. Specifically, existing complex systems were viewed as ineffective whereas Baltimore Job Bank appeared to have achieved excellent results.

Decision codified by: Memorandum for the president from the secretary of labor outlining Department of Labor plans for implementing President Nixon's January 30 directive.

Empirical evidence available to decision-makers: Key results from the Baltimore Job Bank, which had been in operation since May 1968, were discussed in a status report attached to the memorandum codifying this decision. (These results will hereafter be referred to as "Initial Baltimore Data.") The most significant results reported as having been achieved in Baltimore were the following.

"1. Elimination of competition among manpower agencies . . .

"2. A greater body of job orders and openings more suitable to the available labor supply than the agency has ever been able to establish and sustain in the past.

"3. An extensive decentralization of ES staff into the neighborhoods . . . without loss of control . . .

"4. An increase from less than 20 percent to more than 55 percent in referrals *and* placement of disadvantaged jobseekers with no significant loss in the volume of total placements except in professional and clerical placements . . . "

III. Decision: To increase number of Job Banks to be installed by June 30, 1970 from 36 to 55.

Formal date of decision: October 17, 1969

Bases for decision: (a) To speed training of data-processing staff in additional states (key factor in increase was to move from twenty-two to forty states having at least one Job Bank. Each state with one or more Job Banks was required to establish a team to implement computer-aided job-matching systems). This would facilitate development of more sophisticated systems; (b) To expose interviewers and counselors in more cities to ADP, for the purpose of building acceptance of computer-based systems through exposure to such a system; (c) Belief that it was desirable to establish as many Job Banks as possible to help the Employment Service meet its placement role in the FAP Program.[4]

Decision codified by: Memorandum from the assistant secretary of labor for manpower to the manpower administrator.

Empirical evidence available to decision-makers: Only the initial Baltimore data were available at the time this decision was announced. Only four cities, including Baltimore, had had Job Banks operational for more than one month at this time: Hartford had been operating a manual variation of Job Bank, not entirely like those being installed elsewhere, for seven months. Job Banks had been operational for about four months in Portland, Oregon, and in St. Louis.

"The Revised Baltimore Data" (DPDA)[5]

In October 1969, evidence began to appear that there might be some errors in the statistics flowing from the Baltimore Job Bank, The Job Bank tabulation sheet reported many more job openings on hand at the beginning of each recent month than were reported by the Maryland Research and Analysis people using a different computational method. In addition, there was a precipitous decline reported in August 1969 disadvantaged placements on the Job Bank Tabulation sheet.

On October 22, a team from DMMS and the Division of Program Data Analysis (DPDA) visited Baltimore to investigate the questionable data reports. This trip provided some unsettling information. The Job Bank tabulation sheet (used as the basis for the initial Baltimore data referred to above) contained two programming errors. First, since January 1969, openings on hand at the beginning of each month had been computed in such a way that "openings filled" were not deducted. That is, openings reported as being on hand at the beginning of each month were actually the sum of cumulative placements year-to-date, *plus* openings on hand. Hence, although 16,789 openings were reportedly on hand on August 31, the actual number was about 6,500! The significance of this error was substantial: whereas the data showed a very large gain from the comparable 1968 period, there had in fact been a slight drop in openings. However, openings received after the Job Bank opened were substantially greater than before Job Bank. That is, this finding did not negate the initial claim that openings increased substantially after Job Bank.

The second programming error related only to data generated after April 28, 1969. Prior to April 28, "Disadvantaged Applicant" was coded something like "B,D,E," on a certain field. After that date it was accidentally coded "K,L,M, . . . R" in the same field. Hence, after April 28 the number of actions concerning disadvantaged applicants was erroneously reported. The data for May, June, and July happened to be credible, but the August figure was aberrant enough to cause the data to be questioned.

These errors led the National Office to ask the Maryland agency to reexamine all Baltimore Job Bank data and present verified figures. On October 28, these data were mailed to DMMS. The key results for Baltimore Job Bank offices for the first nine calendar months of 1967, 1968, and 1969 are shown in Table 4-1. Recall that the 1967 period was entirely pre-Job Bank, 1969 was post-Job Bank, and 1968 was transitional, i.e., part pre- and part post-.

On November 2, the above findings were made available to the DMMS staff. It was pointed out that these data differed from results claimed earlier for the Baltimore Job Bank in two key respects: First, disadvantaged placements do not constitute "more than 55 percent of total placements."[6] Rather, the correct proportion averaged about 35 percent (still a very high figure, relative to most other areas).

The second key difference was that the new data showed that overall placements had declined about 20 percent from the pre-Job Bank period, and that the drop was spread across a broad spectrum of occupations. The decline in professional and clerical placements was only slightly greater than the average decline. Additional findings, including some statistical analyses of the above results, were made available in DMMS on November 17.

On November 25, the revised Baltimore data were discussed at a DMMS staff meeting. At this meeting it was concluded that the data did not necessarily have negative implications for Job Banks, but no decision was reached concerning further action based on the data.

Table 4-1
Baltimore Job Bank Data (First nine calendar months of each year)

	1967	1968	1969	1967-69 Change
Openings Received	33,982	46,252	46,229	+35%
Placements	25,491	21,240	20,245	−21%
New Applications	59,350	70,093	70,875	+19%
Disadvantaged Placements	1,650	7,955	6,178	+274%
Disadvantaged Percentage of Total Placements	6%	37%	35%	—
Referrals	62,194	59,539	61,354	−10%
Placements by Occupation:				
Professional & Technical	898	671	672	−25%
Clerical & Sales	5,419	4,422	4,167	−23
Service Occupations	8,686	7,433	6,897	−21
Machine Trades	1,037	859	569	−45
Bench Work	2,456	1,622	944	−61
Structural Work	2,969	2,273	2,093	−30
Miscellaneous	3,066	3,102	3,665	+20
Total	25,491	21,240	20,239	−20%

On January 7, 1970, the researchers met with LLA and his immediate superior (MLA) to discuss the Baltimore data and their significance.[7] At this meeting it was agreed that we would undertake a crash program to obtain Baltimore-type data from three or four additional cities, and to analyze these additional data. Following this further work, an interim report would be sent to agency levels above the MLA.

"The Six-City Study"

To facilitate assessing early operating results from the first several Job Bank cities, the Division of Program Data Analysis collected special data for each city

Table 4-2
Performance Data from Six Job Bank Cities

Item	Baltimore			St. Louis			Portland		
	1967	1968	%Δ	1968	1969	%Δ	1968	1969	%Δ
1) Comparison Period	Jan.-Sept.			July-Dec.			July-Dec.		
2) Openings received (000)	34	46	+35	31	28	−8	20	21	+5
3) New applications (000)	59	71	+20	44	44	+1	33	30	−9
4) Nonagricultural Placements (000)	25	20	−20	29	17	−43	14	13	−10
5) HRD intake (000)	11[a]	25	+127	9	7	−27	3	3	−6
6) HRD placements (000)	2[a]	6	+274	8	5	−35	1	3	+142
7) HRD percentage of pl. (6 ÷ 4)	15[a]	30		26	30		10	25	
8) Probability of filling an opening (4 ÷ 2)	.75	.44		.94	.59		.69	.59	
9) Probability of placing an applicant (6 ÷ 3)	.43	.28		.66	.42		.42	.42	
10) Probability of placing an HRD applicant (6 ÷ 5)	.15[a]	.24		.82	.72		.39	1.01	
11) Referrals per placement Total HRD	2.4 INA	3.0 INA		2.0 INA	2.1 INA		2.5 INA	3.2 INA	
12) Nonagricultural referrals (000)	62	61	−1	58	45	−25	30	36	+20
13) SMSA unemployment rate in study period	3.0%	2.9%		3.2%	3.5%		3.3%	3.6%	

[a]Estimated
[b]Includes Casual

from the appropriate state agencies. This study included, in addition to Baltimore, Job Banks in St. Louis, Portland, Seattle, Hartford, and Chicago. For each city, various performance measures were compared for identical periods before and after Job Bank implementation.

The major findings from this analysis are presented in Table 4-2, which is taken directly from the report circulated within the Manpower Administration.

The last section of the report, entitled "Concluding Observations" is reproduced in its entirety here.

Preliminary discussion of these data focused as much on differences among cities as on overall outcomes. The Portland Job Bank is worthy of special attention,

	Seattle			Hartford			Chicago			U.S.		
	1968	1969	%Δ	1968	1969	%Δ	1968	1969	%Δ	1968	1969	%Δ
	Oct.-Dec.			April-Nov.			Oct.-Dec.			Jan.-Dec.		
	2	3	+39	11	16	+45	37	38	+2	8096	7973	−8
	4	6	+47	21	21	NIL	41	47	+14	10367	9853	−5
	2	1	−34	10	8	−22	29	20	−32	5733	5153	−10
	.1	.3	+143	2	5	+106	INA			1801	1656	−8
	NIL	.1	+388	2	2	+13	INA			1104	1015[a]	+12
	1	8		21	30		INA			16	20	
	.69	.33		.97	.52		.78[b]	.52[b]		.68	.69	
	.42	.18		.49	.39		.71[b]	.42[b]		.55	.52	
	.13	.27		.89	.49		INA			.61	.61	
	INA	6.0		3.3	3.5		INA	INA		2.2	2.3	
	INA	INA		INA	INA		INA	INA		2.1	INA	
		INA		34	29	−16	INA			1295	1199	−8
	2.9%	4.7%		3.0%	2.4%		2.5%	2.7%		DNA		

[a]The correct number is 1296, and the 1968-69 change is 15%. Both the incorrect number and percent change were in the original report.

because the Portland data are most encouraging, and because Portland is organized in a radically different form from the other Job Banks. (Interviewers continue to take orders and remained specialized by occupation.)

It is possible to argue that Portland's relatively good placement record is related to continuing the practice of having placement interviewers take orders. However, the increased referral to placement ratio in Portland goes against this argument. As noted earlier, only in Portland did referrals increase, and it is this factor that probably accounts for the relatively good placement record.

Many additional observations might be made about differences among cities, but these are left for discussion to avoid pre-judgment of the results.[8]

The results of the "Six-City Study" were available to LLA on March 2, 1970. On March 9, his staff formally discussed the findings. It was generally agreed that the data were cause for concern, and that the Portland results might be worth digging into, because they were so superior to the outcomes in other cities. At this staff meeting, LLA took the lead in being analytical and chided staff members who made efforts to explain away the results.

On March 16, the "Six-City Study" was discussed with MLA and members of his staff. At this meeting, LLA proposed that we take three actions, based on these data: (1) send the data up the agency ladder to ULA; (2) stop telling cities how to organize Job Banks, in the hope that better organizational designs would emerge; and (3) collect more data. There appeared to be general agreement on these three points.

On March 19, a copy of the "Six-City Study" was forwarded to ULA, together with a brief interpretive memo. Later in March a summary table was sent by ULA to the manpower administrator who in turn forwarded the report to the assistant secretary for manpower (hereafter referred to as ASM(1) or ASM(2), depending on who was the incumbent).

"First Job Bank Interview Study"[9]

During February and March 1970, the present researchers and two outside consultants conducted an interview study in four Job Bank cities: Baltimore, St. Louis, Portland, and Seattle. Employment Service management, and a sample of employers, Community Agencies (CAs), and Employment Service staff were interviewed in each city. The main findings of this study, available to DMMS and OSS staff in March 1970, were the following:

1. Concerning Community Agency Involvement:
   (a) In no city do CAs make over one-half of 1 percent of Job Bank placements
   (b) Virtually no CA openings are put in Job Banks
   (c) There is evidence that CAs tend to make poor referrals
   (d) Nearly all CAs continue to handle the bulk of their placement operation in the same manner as before Job Bank.

2. Concerning Employer Views of Job Bank:
    (a) Overall, employers indicated no significant shift in level of use of the Employment Service in the post-Job Bank period.
    (b) Three-fifths of the employers contacted knew about Job Bank, whereas two-fifths had not heard of it.
    (c) Employers were generally satisfied with the promptness of referrals, and one-third perceived improvement in the post-Job Bank period.
    (d) There was significant employer criticism of the changes in Employment Service organization associated with establishing Job Banks in those cities that had adopted the Baltimore model. Only in Portland, which had not adopted the Baltimore model, did employers fail to criticize the change in organization. It should be noted that these results parallel and confirm the findings of the "Six-City Study."

3. Concerning ES Management and Staff Views:
    (a) The interviews with Job Bank management and staff yielded many constructive suggestions for improving Job Bank operations. However, only one performance-related generalization of note emerged from these interviews: two-thirds of the ES Staff interviewed believed Job Bank leads to improved service for disadvantaged applicants, whereas less than a majority believe other applicants and employers are served better in Job Bank than previously.

"First Hartford JBOR Data"

The first Job Bank Operations Review (JBOR) data were received in DMMS in mid-March. An analysis of these data (from Hartford) was available to LLA and MLA on March 20 and was forwarded to ULA on March 31. Because these data referred only to one city for one month, they did not have policy significance. However, the discussion accompanying the data showed that JBOR had considerable operational value, and thus may have made USTES administrative personnel more aware of, and receptive to, the JBOR data.

There are two pieces of evidence that top-level USTES administrators became more aware of the existence and value of the JBOR as a result of the memorandum developed by the present authors showing how operating managers could exploit JBOR data for their own use. First, we were asked to meet with USTES placement personnel to tell them how JBOR data could be used by operations people. Second, LLA mentioned that the memo on the Hartford JBOR data had caught the attention of his superiors.

IV. Decision: To expand Job Bank coverage to as many additional cities with SMSA populations of a quarter-million as can be operational by June 30, 1970, and which are outside the fifty-six city target goal.
Formal date of decision: Approximately April 2, 1970.

Basis for decision: Apparently to help come as close as possible to meeting June 30, 1970 numerical goal of fifty-six cities.

Decision codified by: Unknown. Noted in April 14 "Job Bank Biweekly Report No. 12" (covering period March 23-April 3). Referred to as ASM(1)-Manpower Administrator-ULA decision.

Empirical evidence available to decision-makers: (a) "Initial Baltimore Data"; (b) "Revised Baltimore Data"; (c) "Six-City Study"; (d) "First JBOR Data"; and perhaps (e) "First Interview Study."

V.   Decision: Recommend several small changes in the organization of Community Agency participation in Job Banks.

Formal date of decision: May 19, 1970.

Basis for decision: To enhance the effectiveness of CA involvement in Job Banks, with a view toward improving efforts to aid the disadvantaged generally.

Decision codified by: Memorandum from MLA to ULA.

Empirical evidence available to decision-makers: The decision to recommend changes in the organization of CA participation in Job Banks was based explicitly on the findings of the first Job Bank interview study. The fact that these results showed that CA participation was actually minimal and that it was *not* generally the case that "competition among manpower agencies has been eliminated" (as the initial Baltimore Report indicated) led to recommending these changes.

VI.   Decision: To expand to all 111 SMSAs with over 250,000 population and at least two local offices by June 30, 1971.[10]

Formal date of decision: May 29, 1970.

Basis for decision: Staff paper, "Phased Implementation Progression for Computer-Assisted Manpower Operations Network." (PIP)

Decision codified: Uncertain. Meeting on May 29, 1970 with ASM(1), the manpower administrator, ULA, MLA, LLA.

Empirical evidence available to decision-makers: (a) "Initial Baltimore Data"; (b) "Revised Baltimore Data"; (c) "Six-City Study"; and perhaps (d) First JBOR Data; and (e) "First Interview Study."

Note: At the beginning of June 1970, the present researchers ended their assignments in DMMS. Our contract to analyze JBOR data and report back our findings to the Manpower Administration had a beginning date of June 15, 1970. Hence, we maintained continuity of contact although we were no longer in as close a relation to Job Bank decisions and progress as we had been during the previous year.

Note: July 3, 1970 ASM(1) was appointed associate director, Office of Management and Budget. The manpower administrator was then appointed as the new assistant secretary of labor for manpower.

"Preliminary Analysis of JBOR Data"
(DMMS)

LLA's staff conducted analyses of JBOR data, over and above the analyses developed by us. The first such analysis was written up in a paper dated November 1, 1970. The data related to Buffalo, Syracuse, Columbus, Memphis, Birmingham, and Little Rock.

The author of the study noted two reservations concerning the data used for the analysis: (1) the pre- and postperiods covered different months of the year. Hence, seasonal factors are not controlled for; and (2) postdata are for months immediately after implementation, when operations are unlikely to be normal.

Despite these reservations, LLA used the data to cast light on answers to key questions concerning the impact of Job Bank on Employment Service operations. The findings of this study were the following.

1. Openings received nearly doubled between pre- and postperiods.
2. Referrals increased 20 percent.
3. Placement decreased 5 percent, although LLA questions these data.
4. First-day service on job orders decreased some, but no other significant change in time to fill openings.
5. Community Agency participation in Job Banks is minimal, with CAs contributing less than one-half of 1 percent of all placements.
6. Service to disadvantaged applicants improved markedly. Referrals increased 60 percent and placements 23 percent. Further, there was shift toward a greater percentage of disadvantaged being placed in higher-wage jobs.

Note: At Atlanta Biregional meeting, November 4, 1970, one of LLA's staff members asked if any cities were still using decentralized order-taking. One said they were, and the staff member said "this makes us very unhappy, as all orders should be taken centrally."

We noted at lunch that this statement was contrary to the LLA-MLA decision (March 16, 1970) based on "Six-City Study" to let states use variations in organization. LLA agreed, but the staff man said "I never heard of this. We've always insisted on central order-taking."

"General Accounting Office Baltimore
Employer Study" (GAO)

In Autumn 1970, the General Accounting Office (GAO) completed a study based on questionnaires mailed to 329 Baltimore employers. A total of 200 employers (61 percent) returned the completed questionnaire.

On balance, the GAO study added little to previous knowledge concerning Job Banks. The major new findings were the following.

1. Few employers felt harassed by the overall level of job order solicitation prior to Job Bank.
2. Few employers saw over-referrals as a problem either pre- or post-Job Banks.
3. Most employers found applicants referred by the ES to be generally qualified for the positions for which they were referred.

Note: On November 30, 1970, MLA told one of the authors that no decisions concerning Job Banks had been made since June.

Note: On December 8, 1970 Arthur Burns (Federal Reserve Board Chairman) made a widely publicized speech on anti-inflation plans. Among other things, he urged "a more aggressive pace in establishing computerized Job Banks." The associated article then went on to refer to the Job Bank Program as "a program that Administration men say is finally coming close to its goals."

"Office of Technical Support Interview Study" (OTS)

In December 1970, the Division of Occupational Analysis and Employer Services, Office of Technical Support, carried out interviews with a total of ninety-eight employers in nine Job Bank cities. Although the focus of the interviews was on "what employers want from the Employment Service," some information specifically relevant to Job Banks emerged from the study. The replies indicated that employers would like the following things, each of which Job Bank affects for better or worse.

1. Closer contact with ES interviewers.
2. Personal touch and industry setup should be reestablished in Job Bank system.
3. ES interviewers should be more knowledgeable of employer requirements. Generalists not as capable as specialists.
4. Better screening of applicants.
5. Prompter service.
6. CA job development should be reduced.

"The Relation between Job Bank Organization and the Skill Mix of Openings Received"

At a meeting on March 10, 1971 with LLA and members of his staff, we discussed data concerning the relation between various Job Bank organizational variables and the skill mix of openings received. This study had been undertaken in response to ASM(2)'s request to ULA-OPER on October 12, 1970 asking that our research cover employer reactions to Job Bank.

We reported that the JBOR data appeared to confirm the specific concerns expressed in ASM(2)'s memo: (1) employers file fewer higher-skill vacancies where order-taking is nonspecialized; (2) employers file fewer higher-skill vacancies where interviewers are not specialized; and (3) employers file fewer higher-skill vacancies where cities have high Community Agency participation in Job Bank.

The basic response to these findings by LLA was that "authority for implementing your proposals (for specialized order-taking and interviewing, and for minimizing CA participation in Job Banks) is widely dispersed within USTES. You really need to meet with lots of other people besides us." Those with authority over the people with whom we needed to meet, i.e., MLA, ULA and ASM(2) did not attend this meeting.

"Analysis of JBOR Data for 16 Job Banks"
(DMMS)

On March 26, 1971 LLA's staff published its second report on its own findings based on JBOR data. In a cover memo conveying the report to these researchers, LLA noted, "I'm a little disturbed at some of the findings but note with some relief that the apparent decline in placements is short-lived." The specific conclusions from this study were the following.

1. Openings received were increasing considerably more in Job Bank cities than elsewhere.
2. Referrals increased between the pre- and post-Job Bank periods.
3. Placements fell in Job Bank cities, but there is some evidence that the decline may be transitory.
4. Job Banks do not significantly affect the speed of service on job orders.
5. In the looser labor markets to which the findings relate, disadvantaged referrals and placements have declined.
6. Community Agency involvement in Job Banks is at a very low level.

"The Impact of Job Banks on Employers:
An Analysis of the Evidence to Date"

On May 21, 1971 these authors sent LLA a report summarizing the results of various studies concerning the impact of Job Banks on employers. This report drew on all of the studies previously discussed, plus an interview study conducted by us in four cities in spring 1971. In total, these studies provide interview or questionnaire data from more than 400 different employers in thirteen cities. The conclusions stated in this report were the following.

1. Job Banks have not affected overall employer *use* of the Public Employment Service.
2. Strong employer criticisms of certain aspects of Job Banks (poor screening of referrals, depersonalization) emerge in every study.

The report concluded by recommending using specialization of referral and order-taking units, and down-playing Community Agency involvement.

Note: An October 19, 1971 memo from ULR-OPER to ASM(2) announced the agenda for our scheduled 11-18-71 meeting. One comment in the memo was that "at our request, Ullman and Huber also looked into the effects of the Job Banks on employer use of the ES. They will report their findings." From this memo, we infer that our March 10, 1971 material responding to ASM(2)'s October 12, 1970 request had not been fed back as far as ASM(2).

"An Interim Analysis of JBOR Data"

On November 17, 1971 the researchers reported on the results of the first large-scale analysis of JBOR data. Present at a preliminary meeting were MLA, LLA's deputy, LLR-OPER, and MLR-OPER.

MLA argued that our negative findings regarding goal attainment, presented outside of the context of PIP, would be viewed at the top of the MA as very distressing and that we should report only to ULA. ULA would then decide what to do with the data. MLR-OPER agreed with MLA.

After some discussion, it was agreed to meet with ULA and his staff in December, after reworking the paper to emphasize the organizational recommendations. The rationale for meeting only with ULA was that he had authority to make all of the recommended changes.

"Improving the Operation of Local Job Banks"

The revised November paper was discussed with USTES and MA research and evaluation staff members on December 15 and 16, 1971. The findings reported at these sessions were essentially those contained in Chapter 3.[11]

At the December 15 meeting with LLA, LLA's deputy, MLA, and MLR-OPER attending, MLR-OPER asked LLA what he intended to do with our findings. LLA said "we will add our conclusions and disseminate the results (about optimal organization). We can't really evaluate the overall program until we have the right organization in every Job Bank." LLA's deputy supported this position, saying "I'm not upset by these results. Some things work better than other things, so put them in." One official expressed concern that making the results public would lead to bad reaction from ASM(2). He noted that "the pressure to implement was so great, we didn't have time to experiment."

The December 16 meeting was attended by LLA, ULA, MLR-OPER, and ULR-OPER. ULA said USTES should look more closely at the eighteen cities on which our conclusions were based, in order to develop more certainty as to what works best. He also asked us to do some additional analysis, which we subsequently did. One key administrator indicated that he was worried about general findings regarding average results. He said "when we formally get this report, we have to share it with the Agency head. He is going to be upset by the results."

"Improving the Operation of Local Job Banks:
A Further Look"

On March 24, we reported back on the results of our further analyses, some of which had been proposed by USTES officials at the December meetings. The meeting was attended by LLA, MLA, MLR-OPER, ULR-OPER, and some other DOL personnel interested in the study.

There was very little discussion of the incremental findings (concerning number of local offices in a Job Bank and procedures for verifying referrals). The main item was the LLA announcement that a program letter containing essentially our recommendations was going to the field.[12]

"An Evaluation of Results and Effectiveness
of Job Banks" (Ultrasystems)

In March 1972 the final report from the Ultrasystems Study of Job Banks became available. This study reached the following conclusions concerning general Job Bank performance.

1. Job Banks consistently are doing more efficiently, and on a better organized basis, certain basic tasks in job order processing and referral control than was previously possible before Job Bank inception.
2. The Job Bank concept provides an excellent management information system for use at local, state, and even national level, for its own evaluation as well as contribution to overall Employment Service performance accountability.
3. In cities with a self-service Job Bank mode, job applicants for the first time have an independent insight into the specifics of the available job market.

4. Community Agencies in the cities visited, whether officially or unofficially cooperating with the Employment Service in the Job Bank system, are not yet deriving all potential benefits from the Job Bank and agency personnel do not view the Job Bank system as supportive of their goals and needs.

5. Job Banks have, for the first time on a large scale, broken the traditional relationship between the Employment Service and employers and have forced, by the very nature of Job Bank implementation and operating philosophy, a critical group of Employment Service staff to focus on the applicant and his needs.

6. Ultrasystems found a prevailing negative image of certain Job Bank procedures to staff outside of Job Bank Central who view Job Bank Central as an entity demanding previously unnecessary man-hours of input effort and possessing an imperious and impersonal communication approach.

7. Even allowing for veteran preferences, NABS, categorical program priorities and other policy or practice limitations, Job Banks offer the potential for more equitable job order exposure to all applicants than ever before.

8. Many official and unofficial expectations of a major positive effect of Job Banks on basic Employment Service productivity measures, such as job order quantity, placement ratios, and the like, have not been realized and perhaps would not have been postulated if there had been a clear understanding of how the Job Bank role would evolve within the Employment Service. It is solely an operating tool and, as designed and presently installed, can only assist with, but not of itself create or fill, job opportunities for ES clients.

9. In general, the main users of Job Bank, employers and job applicants, have not perceived particular change in the quality of service from the Employment Service in the cities visited. Employment Service staff, though they have accepted Job Bank and are trying to work with it, perceive much change, not only in procedures but in the necessity to produce paper work and contribute to statistical tasks without feedback to them on the purpose or potential benefit to their role.

10. A consistent pattern of inadequate staff and cooperating agency training before and after Job Bank installation was found in almost every city visited.

11. Job Bank installations have mandated certain "law and order" steps in improving subsystems of the Employment Service processes such as updating employer files, accurate completion of referral transaction information, reorganization of applicant files, and the like. Too often, this did not, but should have, taken place in advance of the Job Bank operational date.

12. Employment Service management in all cities indicated that most of the

significant public and community relations effort had taken place with regard to Job Bank at the time of its inception. On a continuing basis, ERRs have been "selling" the Employment Service with Job Bank as a beneficial and attractive feature.

13. The movement toward statewide Job Bank implementation needs further controlled experimentation and study in detail.

Concerning the three primary goals ascribed to Job Bank by Ultrasystems, the conclusions were the following.[13]

1. The Job Bank system is meeting its goal of dissemination of Job Order information to Employment Service offices on an overall basis.

2. The Job Bank concept, by its very nature, increases the *probability* of unnecessary referrals due to the wider dissemination of Job Order information. Thus the goal of *elimination* of such referrals is probably unrealistic. However, Ultrasystems found in almost every city what appear to be quite specific control methods and procedures that have been set up to work this problem.

3. Although it is a stated goal of the Job Bank concept to eliminate excessive and wasteful job solicitation visits to employers, there was no specific attempt by Job Bank procedures to control or limit such solicitation in any of the cities visited.

"Findings Concerning the Design and Performance of Local Job Banks: Final Report to U.S. Employment Service Management"

On June 26, a final meeting was held to discuss our total findings and recommendations concerning Job Banks with USTES and OPER officials. The meeting was attended by LLA and some of his staff, MLA's deputy, ULA, LLA-OPER, MLR-OPER, ULR-OPER, and other DOL personnel interested in the study.

We noted that four of our recommendations (specialization of order-taking and referral units, emphasis on employer relations, interviewer access to openings lists, and emphasis on first-day service) had been transmitted to the state agencies via TESPL 2726. We then said we would like USTES's reaction to our other four recommendations (minimizing CA involvement, encouraging a relatively large number of offices in each Job Bank city, restudy verification procedures, and continuing JBOR-type data). ULA said they would take a closer look at the recommendations that Community Agency involvement in Job Banks be minimized, and indicated that it was still possible that they would act on this recommendation. He then asked the researchers how they would implement this recommendation, given that an important client group (disadvantaged applicants) would appear to be adversely affected by such a change.

It was the consensus of the USTES staff that some form of centralized telephone verification procedure was necessary in Job Bank, but that further study might lead to improved procedures. It was pointed out that the mail system has been shown to be too slow and that interviewer verification produces too many phone calls to employers. It was further argued that referral verification was not a very productive way to improve or maintain employer relations. The recommendation concerning continuing JBOR was not discussed due to lack of time.

We noted that, although we believe we have good data on the impact of our research findings concerning Job Bank organization we had no information at all concerning the effect, if any, of our findings regarding Job Bank goals achievement. We then asked what effect these findings had had, and whether they had been communicated above the level of USTES.

ULA asked for an example of a Job Bank goal. When we suggested "reduce frictional unemployment" as an example, he said (1) that he had not communicated this finding to anyone above him in the DOL hierarchy and (2) that they really had not expected Job Bank to have much of an impact on frictional unemployment, at least not in the short run. Further discussion of Job Bank goal achievement led us to conclude that none of the goal findings had been communicated to levels above USTES, although this was not explicitly stated.

There was some discussion concerning the actual goals of Job Banks and the time period in which these goals could be expected to be achieved. ULA noted that Job Banks were a major change in a system, and that it was unreasonable to expect the program to have important effects in less than five to ten years.

ULA said he would have further discussions with his staff concerning our recommendations, and would let us know what was decided and if any additional input from us was desired. He noted that while our findings were useful, they really raise additional questions. For example, perhaps office manager quality is what really matters in determining Job Bank performance.

"A Study of a Study of Job Banks"

On June 30, 1972, fifteen copies of a preliminary draft of the present report were forwarded to MLR-OPER who was responsible for administering this study. A number of events took place between submission of this version and August 31, 1972 when the present and final version was submitted.

1. The copies were circulated to several Department of Labor administrators for their review and comment. A number of suggestions concerning style, format, and a change in title were made and incorporated into the final

version, but no questions concerning the facts or conclusions included in the report were raised.

2. On August 7, the authors were informed that OPER would like us to discuss our report with ASM(2).

3. On August 23, the authors met with ASM(2), LLA's deputy, ULA's deputy, MLR-OPER, and ULR-OPER.

The authors have no way of knowing if this meeting was scheduled as a natural sequel to the June 26 meeting, just discussed, or as a consequence of our preliminary draft of the present report.

After a very brief review of the conclusions contained in Chapter 3 of this report and discussed with the USTES administrators at the June 26 meeting, the discussion turned, as it had in the June 26 meeting, to the question of Job Bank goals. ASM(2) stated that he had always felt that the goal of the Job Bank Program was to increase placements and to improve service to special groups such as veterans and the disadvantaged. ULR-OPER added "also to decrease frictional unemployment." ASM(2) agreed that this was a goal but felt that it flowed from increasing placements.

After a brief review of the conclusions concerning the effect of feedback on the program administrators and the program itself, the ASM(2) observed: "We don't want to be told everything, but maybe we need to do a better job of letting people know what we want to know." After noting our conclusion that negative feedback concerning program performance had not had any effect, ULR-OPER asked what actions we would have diagnosed as evidence of an effect. The three possibilities discussed were the following:

1. A strong impetus for program improvement.

2. An absence of pronouncements from high officials that the Job Bank Program was achieving success in meeting its goals.

3. A redirection of resources from the Job Bank Program to some other program designed to accomplish the same goals.

Conclusions Concerning the Effect of Feedback on Program Administrators: An Interpretation of the Job Bank Experience

This section presents the conclusions we have derived from the preceding section and from our other observations of the Job Bank Program and its administration. Each conclusion is briefly stated, and then the supporting data from this study is presented, as well as some comparable findings of other researchers. Finally, the implications of the conclusion for researchers and for program administrators is discussed.

(1) Conclusion. The administrators of the Job Bank Program desired, sought, and sometimes acted upon recommendations for improving Job Banks.

Supporting Data

a. At a January 7, 1970 meeting, the MLA urged the researchers to study Job Banks for the purpose of improving their operation. He said that "evaluation should tell us how to make programs work, not just that programs are no good."

b. On April 24, 1970 LLA wrote to MLR-OPER urging that the present research be supported. LLA was completely aware of the purpose of the research.

c. On May 19, 1970 MLA wrote a memo to ULA recommending several small changes in the organization of Community Agency involvement in Job Banks. This memo was a direct consequence of the "First Job Bank Interview Study" conducted by the present researchers in the spring of 1970.

d. The fact that USTES administrators encouraged us to conduct the two interview studies is itself evidence of their desire for information concerning ways to improve Job Banks.

e. TESPL 2726, dated April 21, 1972 recommends several changes in Job Bank organization. The TESPL states explicitly that these recommendations are based on the findings of our study and other studies.

Related Findings from Other Studies. A general conclusion obtained by Freeman and Sherwood in their examination of evaluation programs was that such programs have played a very small role in the modification, expansion, or termination of governmental programs.[14] There has been little evidence since that this conclusion needs to be changed. Perhaps our finding that the officials did act on our recommendations does not follow the usual pattern. We examine this question further in Chapter 5. With respect to our findings that the administrators desired and sought recommendations for improvement, we note the experience and comments of Weiss and Rein.

At the very beginning program administrators hoped that the research group might contribute to policy formulation through the development of relevant information, and later, Some administrators found it difficult to accept that the program evaluation work of the research group could only be prepared after the program ended, and thought the research should at least produce hints of what was right or wrong while there was still time to change.[15]

Implications for Researchers. It is possible for researchers to have an impact on operating programs. Hence, researchers should be encouraged to work in the area of program assessment.

Implications for Administrators. The results of analytical studies can be an aid in administering programs. Consequently, administrators should be open to the results of such studies.

(2) Conclusion. The higher administrators in the MA were consciously predisposed to be relatively insensitive, with respect to action-taking, to feedback concerning negative findings. We believe that this is a consequence of the more general conclusion that the effect of feedback is a function of whether it is relevant to an immediately forthcoming decision.

Supporting Data. One of the researchers occasionally had informal contact with some top MA officials. The following quotes, which occurred on these occasions, are included because we believe they have important implications for administrators and researchers.

We decided Job Bank was a good idea, and we haven't seen enough to make us change our minds. You have to make a decision and stay with it for a couple of years, unless you get really strong evidence that you should change. (An Aide to the assistant secretary for manpower, May 1970)

Things come at you so fast, you make the key decisions and then stay with them until it becomes very clear the decision needs changing. (A top Manpower Administration official, June 1970)

Related Findings from Other Studies. For a very interesting documentation of the intermittent character of decision-making, see Gore.[16] Shulberg and Baker noted the same point.[17]

Implications for Researchers. In order to be effective, the feedback of evaluative data must fit the decision-making timetable of the organization. The overall outcome of our feedback efforts can be interpreted in light of this, i.e., organizational findings were used because it was time to reconsider Job Bank organization. However, overall findings were not useful because the overall decision concerning the program was not up for review. The results were simply not timely. (It is interesting to speculate as to what decision would have been made initially had the "Revised Baltimore Data" and/or the "Six-City Study" been available at the time the initial Job Bank decision was reached in March 1969.)

Implications for Administrators. Although we hesitate to generalize from a single example, the predisposition of the top MA officials to continued commitment to Job Banks has an important implication for lower-level MA administrators and for Job Banks themselves. The USTES officials would not have been so hesitant about sending unfavorable data up the hierarchy if they had been aware that such data would not have caused the program decision to be reversed. It seems likely that the main results of thorough airing of the "Revised Baltimore Data" and the "Six-City Study" in the spring of 1970 would have led to a much earlier shift toward the organizational forms proposed in TESPL 2726 in April 1972. Playing down these data served only to maintain less desirable organizational forms, not to assure continuation of the program.

(3) Conclusion. The administrators were inclined to accept facts and implications associated with positive findings and not to accept those associated with negative findings.

Supporting Data

a. Initial and dramatically positive results from a six to nine-month period in Baltimore, Maryland (the agency that first conceived of, designed, implemented, and advocated a Job Bank) were accepted without apparent question by six levels of DOL administration, beginning with LLA and ending with the secretary of labor. Evidence for "accepting without apparent question" was that they were communicated to President Nixon without significant qualification on March 19, 1969. On the other hand, when information became available that some of these initial results were in error, and that Baltimore performance had actually declined on some dimensions, the results were not accepted by LLA as generalizable. Rather, after a delay of approximately two months, a study was initiated in several other cities (the "Six-City Study") in order to get a clearer picture of the effects of Job Banks.

b. The March 19, 1969 memorandum from the secretary of labor to President Nixon stated that "there is some promise of reduction in frictional unemployment," and the research proposal of the present researchers, approved by LLA and MLA, listed the goal of reducing frictional unemployment first on its list of goals whose performance was to be studied. On November 17, 1971 and December 15 and 16, 1971, the researchers reported that according to their measure of frictional unemployment, the Job Banks had not reduced frictional unemployment and may have increased it. In the November 17, 1971 meeting, MLA asked us to move this objective from first to last in our discussion, and then questioned whether we should report at all on this goal. He noted that "the frictional unemployment goal came from an effort to make [a high administration official] happy." In the June 26, 1971 meeting, ULA noted that he and other initiators of Job Banks had not really expected any consequent reduction in unemployment, at least not in the short run.

c. At the feedback meetings of November 17, 1971 and December 16, 1971, MLA argued that the finding that the referral to placement ratios (the average number of applicants referred to a job before a placement is made) had increased dramatically was not necessarily bad, if it resulted in more placements overall. The facts that placements had not increased and that one of the stated goals of Job Banks was to provide more efficient service seemed to be ignored in the nonacceptance of this negative finding.

    d. An aide to the ASM(1) told one of the researchers that he and ASM(1) had looked briefly at the table and memo concerning the "Six-City Study," but had not acted on it because "the data didn't make any sense."

Related Findings from Other Studies. We can only speculate on the causes of these actions and attitudes, but some possible explanations do appear in the literature. These administrators believed in the worth of this program for several reasons, among them the early, positive (and somewhat erroneous) findings concerning the Baltimore Job Bank. In this regard, Ference notes that "information that is inconsistent with information acquired earlier in the problem-solving process is likely to be rejected."[18] Pitz, in laboratory research has arrived at findings supportive of ours and of Ference's generalization, as did the researchers associated with Webster.[19,20]

In some instances, professional considerations may be an explanation. Campbell has observed that "in the present political climate, reformers and administrators achieve their precarious permission to innovate by overpromising the certain efficacy of their new programs. This traps them so that they cannot afford to risk learning that the programs were not effective."[21] Downs summarizes several pages of discussion with the proposition that "officials' perceptions will operate so as to partially screen out data adverse to their own interests, and magnify those favorable to their interest."[22] Thus two possible explanations for some of the observed behavior are the rather pervasive disinclination to change one's opinion about anything and the professional inclination to perceive what is supportive more quickly than that which is not supportive.

Implications for Researchers. Evaluative feedback, if it is negative, should be coupled with an analytical analysis of causes of nonperformance and recommendations for corrective action.

Implications for Administrators. Administrators should be aware of their natural tendency to disregard or discount negative information and to assign too high a credence to positive findings. (The original Baltimore results are an important instance of the latter.)

(4) Conclusion. The administrators were inclined to communicate positive findings and not to communicate negative findings.

Supporting Data

    a. The initial and dramatically positive results from Baltimore were communicated widely, e.g., to President Nixon in the memo from the secretary of labor and to all state employment security agencies in a program letter, (TESPL2525) and in these cases with several pages of elaboration and recommendations for action based upon the results. On the other hand, the revised and much less encouraging Baltimore data and the relatively discouraging data included in the "Six-City Study" were forwarded only as far as the assistant secretary of manpower, and then only as a relatively brief memo and a summary table.

b. On November 14, 1969, TESPL2525, which included the initial and positive Baltimore data, was released to the state agencies, even though on October 22, 1969 the National Office study team had ascertained that these data were incorrect and on November 2 the revised, correct, and much more mixed Baltimore data were available to LLA.

c. The researchers had arranged to report their negative findings concerning the relative achievement of the Job Bank goals to ASM(2) on November 18, 1971. On the previous day they met with MLA and his staff who argued so strongly against reporting these findings that the researchers agreed to cancel the meeting. (Two arguments were made for not meeting with ASM(2): (1) ASM(2) was not prepared to receive such information out of context; (2) USTES staff were in position to make decisions concerning all of our recommendations. Hence, it was not necessary to meet with the assistant secretary.) It should also be noted MLR-OPER, who funded most of this study, agreed with MLA that it could be bad to give negative data to the assistant secretary without at least putting it in the context of the Phased Implementation Progression.

d. The researchers reported their negative findings regarding the relative achievement of the Job Bank goals to ULA and others on December 16, 1971. ULA expressed some concern over communicating these results upwards, saying for instance that "when I *formally* get this report, I *have* to share it with the assistant secretary. [Emphases are the author's.] I would rather wait until February to do this." ULA also expressed some concern over who had received copies of the report then being presented, indicating that enemies of the Job Bank Program would use these findings to attack it.

e. The Job Bank study by Ultrasystems, which reached more positive conclusions concerning Job Banks than did our research, was summarized in a formal meeting with the assistant secretary. No such meeting was suggested to the present researchers by the USTES administrators, although one was arranged by OPER administrators after the preliminary draft of this report was submitted.

The patently unequal handling of "good news" and "bad news" in the various levels of the Manpower Administration has had the general effect of leading to overstating the achievements of local Job Banks.

a. The initial Baltimore results were commented on by Ruttenberg in 1970, in speaking hopefully of the promise of Job Banks: "Although total placements (in Baltimore) have remained the same, placement of disadvantaged applicants has increased about 250 percent, from less than 20 percent to more than 50 percent of total placements in the area covered by the Job Bank."[23] (The book in which this quote appears has had wide circulation. Nowhere have we seen quotes of the later more reliable, but less cheering results.)

b. On December 7, 1970 Federal Reserve Board Chairman Arthur Burns urged in a speech at Los Angeles that the administration adopt "a more aggressive pace in establishing Job Banks."[24] The article reporting the speech then noted that the Job Bank program was "a program that Administration men say is finally coming close to its goals." According to our understanding, Mr. Burns had been an enthusiastic supporter of the National Computer Job Bank idea at the very beginning of the Nixon administration. Since no new data other than the "Six-City Study" had become available by December 7, and since the "Six-City Study" findings were so negative, one wonders if Mr. Burns was aware of these new findings at the time of this speech.

c. In June 1972 the secretary of labor announced that job listings and placements had taken a "significant upturn" in recent months. In part, the secretary attributed the upturn to "an expanding network of computerized job banks."[25]

Related Findings from Other Studies. As before, while we can only speculate on the causes of these actions and attitudes, we can perhaps obtain some suggestions from the literature. Thompson offers the following proposition: "Where alternatives are present, the individual is tempted to report successes and suppress evidence of failures." A corollary to that is offered by Downs: "Each individual tends to distort the information he passes upward in the hierarchy, exaggerating those data favorable to himself and minimizing those unfavorable to himself."[26,27] Read summarizes his field study of three major industrial organizations by writing that "individuals in power hierarchies tend to screen information passed upward, and to withhold or refrain from communicating information that is potentially threatening to the communicator."[28]

Rosen and Tesser have some evidence that people tend not to communicate negative information even when there is no anticipation of an adverse action being taken toward the communicator.[29] They speculate that people simply do not like to carry bad news and consequently observe its effect on the recipient. This could be an explanation of the statements made, by some of the administrators, as to why they did not want our negative findings forwarded to the assistant secretary.

Implications for Researchers. At the beginning of the research project, research-ers should arrange procedures for communicating findings to the highest possible level of the organization responsible for the program being studied.

Implications for Administrators. Administrators should insist that all relevant information should be passed to them, regardless of the positive or negative nature of the data.

(5) Conclusion. Policies were more important determinants of program-related decisions than was information about the effectiveness of the program. (To a considerable extent this conclusion is a consequence of the earlier conclusions. The reader may want to verify this for himself by relating the previously presented supporting data. Nevertheless, there seem to be supporting data for this conclusion that are relatively independent of that from the earlier dis-cussion.)

Supporting Data

a. As far as we know, the decision to develop a national computer-aided job-matching network was based on no more information than that computer matching of men and women for social purposes had been successfully implemented. The administration's desire to reduce unem-ployment and the employment problems of the disadvantaged particularly seem to have been the forces behind this decision and the subsequent decisions to implement Job Banks in thirty-six, then fifty-five, cities.

b. LLA indicated to the Maryland agency (Baltimore Job Bank) that work on the installation of the job-matching system (an expansionary undertaking) should take priority over program work to produce the data needed to evaluate Job Bank contribution (an information-gathering undertaking). This was codified in a memo from the director, Office of Technical Support to the Director, Office of Systems Support, December 12, 1969.

c. One of the recommendations made by these researchers was that Com-munity Agency involvement in Job Banks be minimized. As documented in Chapter 2, the evidence supporting this recommendation was very strong. Despite this evidence, this particular recommendation was not transmitted to the state agencies, because of National Office policies favoring Community Agency involvement in Job Banks.

d. On April 2, 1970 it was decided to implement Job Banks in as many cities with over a 250,000 population as was possible before June 30, 1970, and on May 29, it was decided to implement Job Banks in all the 111 Standard Metropolitan Statistical Areas that had populations over 250,000. These expansionary decisions were made in spite of the fact that the negative to neutral findings of the "Six-City Study" and the First Interview Study were known to at least some of the administrators involved.

e. The above expansion, an implementation of general policy, eliminated the control cities that were to be used to provide information about the effectiveness of Job Banks.

Implications for Researchers. Researchers should attempt to become aware of policies pertaining to the programs they are considering studying. This is because, if there are firm policies for continuance of certain program aspects, his findings may not have any impact, regardless of their nature. On the other hand, if it is decided to conduct an evaluation, despite strong policies, the researcher will need to be especially persuasive in presenting his findings if he is to have an impact.

Implications for Administrators. There is a danger that subordinates will ignore or devalue recommendations for program alteration or curtailment because of misconceptions concerning the exact nature of or weight to be assigned to particular policies. To minimize this problem, higher-level administrators should be certain that their subordinates have the clearest possible understanding of the natures and weights of particular policies.

The above conclusions primarily concern the impact of feedback on the program administrators. It is through having an impact on administrators that feedback could have an effect on the program itself. Our conclusions with respect to the effect of feedback on the direction and structure of the program follow.

(1) Conclusion. The findings concerning overall goal achievement, which were almost entirely negative, have not had any effect on the Job Bank Program. The primary reasons for this appear to be (a) most of the findings do not appear to have been communicated to persons in position to affect the allocation of resources between Job Banks and competing programs; (b) such findings as have reached those in position to affect the allocation of resources to Job Banks have not been considered by those receiving them to be of consequence sufficient to use as inputs to decisions.

Supporting Data

a. There seemed to be no strong impetus for improving the program. The only improvement-oriented action, based on feedback, was the release of the program letter, TESPL 2726, dated April 1972. We note (1) that program letters contain information and recommendations but are not directives, and (2) some of TESPL's recommendations follow from feedback received as early as March 1970 and the remainder follow from recommendations made in November 1971.

b. As noted earlier, in December of 1970 and in June of 1972 top administration officials publicly suggested that the Job Bank Program was in the process of achieving its goals. Since our feedback was to the contrary, it is doubtful that it was having much of an impact on the program.

c. We are aware of no DOL decision that has diverted resources from the Job Bank Program to other programs designed to achieve the same goals, in spite of the lack of evidence that the program is achieving its goals. While we did not expect this to occur, if it had occurred, it could have constituted evidence that the feedback did have an effect on the program.

(2) Conclusion. The findings concerning Job Bank organization have had an effect on the ES National Office position regarding optimal organization. However, the findings had an impact only when (a) the National Office was already neutral or positive concerning the matter about which data were presented, or (b) the evidence was overwhelming. The latter condition was not always sufficient to lead to adoption of the recommendation: in one matter in which a recommendation was contrary to a policy (to emphasize service to disadvantaged applicants through association with Community Agencies), over-whelming evidence that the policy led to poor performance was not deemed sufficient reason for adopting the organizational recommendation (to minimize [Community Agency] involvement).

Supporting Data. The internal USTES correspondence and TESPL 2726, de-scribed earlier are evidence of an effect from feedback. The discussion in "(5) Conclusion" concerns the influence of policy as a moderator on the effect that can be achieved.

This concludes our review of the effects of feedback. The conclusions and recommendations that follow from it are contained in Chapter 5.

Concluding Observations

This chapter is intended to put the research into perspective and to present some conclusions and recommendations flowing from the total research experience. The chapter consists of three sections. The first contains our ideas concerning the conditions that favor utilization of research findings by program administrators. Implicit in the section are some recommendations for conducting and gaining the maximum benefit from this sort of research. The second section is a discussion of an interesting and unanswered question about research design. The final section contains our ideas about the value of this research effort.

**Conditions Favoring Utilization
of Research Findings**

We mentioned in Chapter 1 and repeat here the observation that research generally seems to have had little impact on program administration. For example, Freeman and Sherwood state: "Certainly it is difficult to point out many instances in which programs actually have been modified, expanded or terminated because of evaluation findings."[1] Besides documenting this assertion, however, the social science literature indirectly suggests that under certain conditions an impact might be achieved. Weiss and Rein focus on problem diagnosis:

Research cannot merely document that the program failed and go on to study a modification of the program; it must identify the causes of failure. In this way the experience can become a basis for designing more effective programs.[2]

Miles, et al., emphasize interaction between the researchers and the administrators:

Survey feedback is a process in which outside staff and members of the organization collaboratively gather, analyze and interpret data that deal with various aspects of the organization's functioning and its members' work lives, and using the data as a base, begin to correctively alter the organizational structure and the members' work relationships.[3]

Shulberg and Baker cite ineffective communications, which have the result that "the administrator alleges that the researchers' findings have been presented in an unnecessarily frustrating and abstract manner.[4] These ideas cause one to wonder about the conditions that might favor utilization of research findings.

It is clear to us that some of our research findings had a documentable impact, whereas other results were apparently completely ignored. We have worked to try to understand the circumstances affecting this difference in impact. Although our identification of these circumstances or conditions is based as much on our impressions as on hard evidence, we list here the situations that in our best judgment enhance the probability that research results will be utilized by program administrators. In some respects they are the guidelines that we would suggest to a researcher or research funding agency desiring to have an impact on a program. The first four were developed from this research experience. The last two are part of the conventional wisdom of field researchers and consultants and were reinforced in our day-to-day observation of our own interaction with Manpower Administration officials from June 1970 to June 1971.

1. Results will be utilized if it is time to make a decision. Decision-making is a periodic rather than a continuous activity.[5] Data available closest to a succeeding decision is most likely to have an impact.[6] It appears to us that the relation between the findings available concerning Job Bank performance and the use to which these findings were put can be understood only if the concept of timeliness is considered.

2. Results are more likely to be utilized if the person receiving the results is in a position to act on them. Our research leads us to believe that administrators have a general reluctance to *send* negative results to higher levels. Hence, the probability of administrative action is directly related to the ability of the person receiving the results to *act* on them.[7]

3. Positive results are more likely to be utilized than are negative results. This follows from the previous statement. Positive results will be passed to higher levels and thus may be acted on at any level. Negative results will tend to get action only if the receiver can act himself.

4. Results will be utilized if they are intuitively appealing to those receiving them. Administrators rely heavily on their early, visceral judgments. Findings that confirmed ideas already held were more quickly accepted than were findings that were contrary to present ideas.

5. Results are more likely to be utilized if there is frequent and meaningful interaction between the administrators and evaluators in the design, implementation, data analysis, and results interpretation of the study. Such interaction increases the quality and relevance of the study and enhances the ability of the two parties to communicate effectively.

6. Results are more likely to be utilized, the more credible those presenting the data are to the administrators. Credibility can presumably be obtained in various ways.

A Possible Model of
Decision-making Structure

We observed that the three administrators with whom we worked, LLA, MLA, and ULA, (1) had the knowledge to judge the worth of our findings concerning optimal design, (2) had the influence or authority to get them accepted within USES and (3) took action in forwarding them as recommendations to the state agencies. On the other hand, we observed that these same administrators took no action on our findings concerning goal achievement. Perhaps this was because they did not want to communicate them to other administrators, but perhaps it was because they did not have the authority or influence to get them accepted or did not have the knowledge that would enable them to make judgments concerning the implied redistribution of funds or manpower from Job Banks to some other manpower-related program.

Consider the administrators above ULA in the DOL hierarchy, i.e., the assistant secretary and the secretary of labor. These men have the knowledge necessary to make judgments concerning redistribution of resources and the influence or authority to implement them. On the other hand, they may be too far removed from the operating levels to judge the worth of findings concerning optimal design or to be very concerned about their implementation.

Perhaps we can generalize these thoughts to the following. For a particular hierarchy of decision-makers and a particular item of feedback information passing upward through the hierarchy, there is a key decision-maker who, as a consequence of his authority and knowledge, chooses either to regard it as diagnostic and to prescribe remedial action or to regard it as evaluative of policy and to review it for possible upward communication. Everyone below him would regard it as evaluative of policy and everyone above him would regard it as diagnostic.[8]

In the cases of both diagnostic and evaluative feedback, it seems reasonable to believe that continual positive feedback would cause researchers to be regarded as useful aides and to be given even more cooperation, and that continual negative feedback would cause researchers to be regarded as auditors and to be given less cooperation. We note that during the duration of this study, the cooperation given us varied little if at all, perhaps because the valence of our feedback was mixed. Clearly this last thought is extrapolative of our experiences in settings other than this study.

If this model of decision-making structure is representative of reality, it suggests an interpretation for the decision-making behavior that we observed. It appeared that our feedback concerning optimal design was regarded by LLA, MLA, and ULA as diagnostic, except for that concerning Community Agency participation, and hence they took remedial action—TESPL 2726. Our feedback regarding goal achievement and Community Agency participation, however, apparently was regarded as evaluative of the policy of expanding the Job Bank Program and was reviewed for possible upward communication.

It follows from the above that for any particular program there are two conceptually different levels in the hierarchy, one of which is responsive to findings concerning program design and the other to findings concerning goal achievement. It may be that a research effort with the dual goals of having an impact both on program design and also on resource allocation is nonideal, in that there are *two* key administrators involved who are located some distance apart in the hierarchy. At this time the implications of this hypothesis are not clear to us, and we would appreciate comments and ideas. One implication might be that if a researcher is to have the confidence and total cooperation of the lower-level program-directing administrators, he must not have the auditing function implied by also reporting to the upper-level administrators.

The above hypothesis suggests that separate research efforts should be used to achieve these separate goals. On the other hand, a single research effort directed toward achieving both goals is clearly more efficient, in terms of data-handling, and may be more effective because the knowledge gained in analyzing one set of data can be useful in analyzing the other. The question is an important one for those persons interested in research on manpower or other social programs, whether they be researchers, program administrators, or funding agencies, and seems worthy of further study.

Value of the Research

Although this research focused on a single manpower program, the study contains findings of general interest and importance to both administrators and social scientists. First, the study demonstrates that under certain conditions, the feedback of research results can have an impact on the administration of programs. This is a somewhat more optimistic conclusion than some others have reached.

The second main value of the study is an enumeration of some of the conditions likely to lead to implementation of research results. These conditions were set forth earlier in this chapter.

The third payoff from the research is that it led to modification of the recommended design of local Job Banks toward a more effective configuration. This was discussed in Chapter 4.

Finally, the study demonstrated the feasibility of an empirical approach to optimum organization design. This subject has long interested both administrators and students of organizations, but the subject has grown in importance in recent years due to the growing number of franchises, holding companies, and other manifestations of organizational replication. Hence, the potential payoff from identifying optimum organizational designs is much greater now than was formerly the case.

Appendixes

Appendix 1: Design and Methodology of the Research

As noted in early chapters, there were three purposes of the overall research effort. Each purpose demanded a separate research design. A summary and overview of these research designs appears in Chapter 2 of this report. In the following sections of this appendix, we describe in more detail the design and methodology associated with each of our three research goals. The problems we encountered are also described because: (1) the problems caused our methodology to be different from what it would have been if the actual research conditions had been more ideal, and (2) researchers learning of our problems here might be more sensitive to the possibility of encountering similar problems in their own program assessments or organizational studies and being forewarned, may be forearmed.

Assessing the Extent of Goal Achievement

The methodology used in assessing goal achievement was discussed in detail on pages 14-16.

Obtaining Performance Data:
Developing and Implementing the Job
Bank Operations Review (JBOR)

One of the authors spent most of his time during his eleven-month tour in the agency developing and implementing the Job Bank Operations Review (JBOR) program. JBOR is the data-collection program developed to provide the basis for an assessment of local Job Banks.

Documentation of the effort put forth to introduce JBOR has two purposes. First, the discussion shows the difficulty of implementing nonstandard procedures in a large bureaucratic organization. Second, an understanding of the degree of care taken to assure successful implementation provides useful background for the subsequent discussion of the shortcomings of the JBOR data ultimately used in the analysis.

Initial Development of JBOR. Prior to the authors' commencing employment in July 1969, the Division of Manpower Matching System (DMMS) staff had done some preliminary design work on a program to collect operating data from Job Banks in order to assess the effectiveness of the Job Bank Program. Given that DMMS had broad responsibility for implementing Job Banks and was not specifically responsible for assessment, it is unusual that the design of an assessment system had been begun in the division. As will be seen, many people in the agency eventually questioned the legitimacy of the DMMS effort to assess its own program.

The explanation of DMMS interest in assessing Job Banks lies in the character and backgrounds of the division chief and his deputy. The division chief, hereafter referred to as LLA, has a staff background, as well as an inquisitive and analytical mind. He once told the authors, by way of explaining his strong interest in assessing his own operating programs, "all through my career, I've wondered how worthwhile the programs I've worked on really were. I promised myself that if I were ever put in charge of a program, I would see to it that I knew whether or not the program was any good."

LLA's deputy's background was primarily in research and statistics areas. He had published several articles, and was generally disposed toward doing research. It was natural for him to work on program assessment at the same time he carried out his operating responsibilities. He had done the initial work on the assessment materials prior to the authors' arrival.

The basic concepts underlying the JBOR design had been spelled out prior to our involvement. Our design work was primarily a continuation of this initial DMMS effort. During the last half of July 1969, one of the authors redesigned the initial system in cooperation with DMMS staff. The basic design approach of beginning with program objectives, developing criteria for determining if the objectives were being realized, and specifying the data needed, was spelled out in all essentials by the end of July 1969.

The one major design change made after July was the deletion of a table, "Work Days Taken to Place Applicants." Initially, this table was included in the belief that pre- and postdata from it would provide a direct measure of the impact of Job Banks on frictional unemployment. The table was deleted after discussions with state agency officials revealed that "Work Days Taken to Place Applicants" could not be determined from existing or readily obtainable operating data. In line with the agreed-upon policy that we would use only data available or needed for operating purposes, this table was abandoned. Ultimately, we decided that we could infer the impact of Job Banks on unemployment through use of data on "time required to fill openings," which was already available. Hence, we do not believe that deletion of this table significantly detracted from our ability to assess this Job Bank goal.

Implementing the JBOR Requirement. The formal implementation of programs directing state agencies to submit data to the National Office requires the approval or comment of various organizations within the Manpower Administration, the State Employment Security Agencies, and the Office of Management and Budget (at the time of this study called Bureau of the Budget, or BOB). This formal approval process, called "clearance," inevitably requires considerable time to complete.

In the case of JBOR (and presumably in most instances where preimplementation data are required) a lengthy delay in collecting data would have emasculated the research design. The rapid rate at which Job Banks were being implemented meant that significant delays in getting JBOR underway would greatly reduce the number of cities for which pre-Job Bank data could be obtained.

In order to mitigate the problem of the delay needed for formal clearance of the JBOR programs, it was decided to move ahead on an informal basis, while at the same time taking the steps needed for formal implementation. The approach taken consisted of working directly with the appropriate technicians in USTES, the Office of Manpower Management Data Systems (OMMDS—which was responsible for implementing data systems and collecting data from the field; this office has subsequently been renamed Office of Financial and Management Information Systems, or OFMIS), and the State Employment Security Agencies. The organizational relationships among these organizations are shown in Figure 1-A. The Bureau of the Budget was kept informed of our activities on an informal basis, in addition to being a part of the formal approval process.

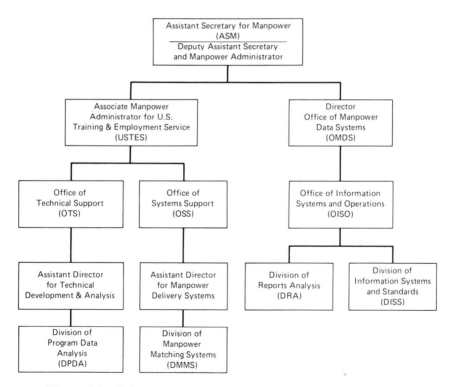

Figure 1-A. Relationship among Various Manpower Administration Organizations Involved in JBOR Development (For Period from July 1, 1969 through June 30, 1970).

Before discussing the specific steps taken in informally implementing JBOR, it should be pointed out that circumstances were especially favorable in this instance for acting informally as well as for expediting formal procedures. First, one of the present researchers had as essentially a full-time assignment the implementation of JBOR. Because the research opportunities associated with JBOR were perceived by him as having substantial professional payoff, he was very highly motivated to be successful in implementing JBOR. Second, because he was an "outsider," who was not really a part of DMMS, the person responsible for JBOR was probably perceived by others within USTES as being less threatening than if he had been a regular member of the staff. This point goes to the matter of the "turf-protecting" instincts of persons in bureaucratic organizations.[1] Third, implementation of JBOR, or a similar design, had the specific backing of the assistant secretary of labor for manpower, ASM(1).[2] Fourth, the present author working on JBOR implementation had been associated with ASM(1) a few years earlier, working as outside consultants to USTES. Knowledge of this relationship may have had an impact on some of those whose cooperation was required in circumventing formal clearance procedures. This is speculative, however, as the researcher at no point consciously played on his earlier acquaintance with the assistant secretary in implementing JBOR, nor was he ever told that this relationship had any effect on the cooperativeness of the persons involved in implementing JBOR.

Obtaining Formal Approval Within USTES. Within USTES, "reporting activities" were the responsibility of the Division of Program Data Analysis (DPDA), Office of Technical Support. Data from the state agencies were gathered through dealings between DPDA and the Research and Analysis or Research and Statistics Departments in the state.

At this time—August 1969—DPDA was involved in the design and implementation of a new reporting system called Employment Service Automated Reporting System (ESARS). ESARS was a major reporting initiative undertaken jointly by USTES, OMMDS, and the state agencies. ESARS was intended to be a comprehensive Employment Service data system, and was scheduled for national implementation in July 1970.

In initial discussions with DPDA on August 22, the DPDA division chief and his immediate superior questioned the legitimacy of the DMMS-JBOR activity. They based their position on three ideas. First, JBOR significantly overlapped the data provided by ESARS; second, additional information was needed if JBOR was to be a stand-in for ESARS prior to ESARS implementation; and third, JBOR was a reporting activity and therefore was not within DMMS area of responsibility.

In rebuttal, we (i.e., these researchers) pointed out that ESARS would not be in place soon enough to provide pre-Job Bank data, and that the capture of post-Job Bank data was necessary to insure comparability between the pre- and postdata. This position was accepted, with the provision that JBOR data would be collected in Job Bank cities only, pre-Job Bank, and for twelve months after implementation of each Job Bank.

It was also agreed that JBOR would be altered to provide the additional data desired by DPDA. Finally, it was agreed that because JBOR data would be used to improve the design of Job Banks and was not primarily a reporting activity, it was legitimate for DMMS to have some involvement in JBOR. Subsequently, DPDA agreed that we should proceed with JBOR informally, in that we were really just checking feasibility and preparing to collect data.

Obtaining Informal State Agency Cooperation. During the next several months the researchers, sometimes accompanied by other DMMS staff, discussed JBOR with staff of several state agencies. As mentioned above, one purpose of these visits was to discuss and perfect the JBOR design. The second purpose was to seek the cooperation of the state agencies in implementing JBOR prior to it becoming a formal requirement. Specifically, where Job Banks had not yet been implemented, we asked state agencies to collect pre-Job Bank JBOR data or take steps to assure that the data could be recaptured. Where Job Banks were operational, we asked that JBOR-type data be provided as soon as possible.

To facilitate state agency JBOR work, DMMS was having a JBOR computer-program package developed as part of the USTES National Office Job Bank Standard Program Package. This set of JBOR programs could be used to generate JBOR tables in nearly every state, whether or not the state had adopted the National Office Standard Program Package. Use of this JBOR Program Package, developed by a National Office consultant, greatly simplified the work required to produce JBOR output.

DMMS offered to provide supplementary budget funds to the state agencies to cover the cost of gathering pre-Job Bank data. The dates and outcomes of the visits to the state agencies were the following, as recorded in trip reports.

1. Ohio (8-12-69). It was agreed that Columbus Job Bank would produce pre- and post-data, beginning in October if JBOR design firm by late August. Columbus was scheduled to open February or March 1970.
2. Missouri-Kansas (8-27-69). It was agreed that it was possible for Missouri (and probably Kansas) to produce pre- and post-data for Kansas City, although no beginning date was promised. Kansas City was scheduled to open in February 1970.
3. Maryland (9-25-69). No agreement on providing JBOR data, as Maryland agency was very busy working on other ADP matters. The agency agreed to consider JBOR implementation. Baltimore had been in operation since May 1968, and the state agency was producing its own set of tables covering operations.
4. Connecticut (9-11-69). Agreement was reached that JBOR would be imple-

mented October 1 in Hartford, New Haven, Bridgeport, and perhaps one or two additional areas where Job Banks are contemplated. Hartford was open, so no pre-data was available there. Bridgeport was scheduled to open April 1970, whereas New Haven was scheduled for June opening.

5. Pennsylvania (9-15-69). No significant pre-data would be provided for Pittsburgh as it was too close to start-up date. They agreed tentatively to collect pre-data later for Philadelphia if National Office would pay significant share of cost, Pittsburgh scheduled to open November 1969. Philadelphia to open April 1970.

6. Regional meetings—Memphis (10-16-69). In addition to visiting individual states, JBOR was discussed at various regional meetings held to discuss various aspects of Job Bank implementation. At this meeting, the Georgia agency agreed to begin collecting pre-data in November for Atlanta, scheduled to open in January 1970. No specific agreements were reached with other participating states (Florida, Kentucky, Mississippi, North Carolina, South Carolina, and Tennessee).

7. Wisconsin (11-12-69). It was agreed that Milwaukee data would be provided for January 1970 and subsequent months. The Milwaukee Job Bank was scheduled for implementation by June 1970.

8. Illinois (11-13-69). It was agreed that Illinois would attempt to submit JBOR data for December 1969 and subsequent months. The Chicago Job Bank Opened in October 1969.

Obtaining Formal Approval Outside USTES. JBOR received final approval within USTES in October and was forwarded to OMMDS. OMMDS then began taking the final steps required to obtain clearance of the program.

In November JBOR was formally cleared with the Research and Reporting Committee (R&R Committee) of the Interstate Conference of Employment Security Agencies (ICESA). The R&R Committee expressed concern about JBOR, centered on four issues: (1) coordination with ESARS requirements; (2) timing the requirement for pre-Job Bank data; (3) cost; and (4) criteria chosen for evaluation.

The views of the R&R Committee were in some instances expressed in pungent prose. Among the comments were "the most hopeful thing here is the introductory statement that 'the review design is currently being rewritten.' "

"We should object violently, and picket, if necessary, to the requirement of preparation of these tables for several months prior to the establishment of the Job Bank. Local offices just do not have the time. . . . "

"From a reporting stand point this will be an operational nightmare."

"It is our strong opinion that the Research and Reporting Committee, ICESA, take a long look at this document and suggest delay in implementation pending the issuance of Job Bank guidelines and full operation of the ESARS system."

Although the above comments may seem caustic, they are in fact representative of the views expressed by the state agency research and statistics people who make up the bulk of the R&R Committee membership.

A response to the R&R Committee objections was prepared, and JBOR was considered to have cleared this committee. At the time we were not especially concerned at the negative reaction from this group. However, as will be seen later, the R&R Committee reaction should have been interpreted as a warning of problems to be encountered in getting full cooperation from the state agencies in providing JBOR data.

In December USTES reviewed the fourth revision of the JBOR documents, and notified OMMDS that formal implementation could proceed. Formal approval by BOB was received early in January.

On January 9, 1970 telegrams were sent from ULA to all regional manpower administrators announcing that General Administration Letter (GAL) 1353 concerning JBOR requirements, would be issued approximately January 15, 1970. GAL 1353 required state agencies to collect JBOR data beginning in February 1970 for cities scheduled to have Job Banks by June 30, 1970. There were fifty-five cities. GAL 1353 is reproduced in Appendix 3.

GAL 1353 directed the state agencies to provide JBOR data. Several special steps were taken to enhance the quantity and quality of the data actually received. By agreement with OMMDS, JBOR reports were routed from the state agencies through OMMDS to DMMS in USTES. OMMDS took responsibility only for seeing that the reports were received on schedule. Special procedures were adopted within DMMS to further monitor the inflow of the data. First, a clerk in DMMS informed OMMDS on the first of each month what additional Job Banks should report that month. Second, the DMMS clerk audited the inflow to be sure that reports were actually being received as scheduled. Third, DMMS checked each report for accuracy and completeness, and prepared a query (Form ES 290) to the state agency covering apparent errors or omissions. The present researchers trained the DMMS clerk in examining the incoming data for omissions and obvious errors.

In the case of JBOR, OMMDS served simply as a conduit and did not monitor the content of the data. In other data-collection programs, OMMDS not only oversees the collection of the data but is also responsible for analyzing and disseminating the data.

Collecting JBOR Data from State Agencies. At the time these researchers left their Manpower Administration assignments in early July 1970, we fully expected to have several months of pre-Job Bank data and comparable post-data from at least forty Job Bank cities. This estimate turned out to be extremely overoptimistic, as we actually obtained usable data for the same time period from twenty-two cities, four of which were subsequently not used for reasons discussed in the subsection, "Obtaining Design Data: The Operations Flow Study," p. 106.[3]

In the following section we describe and analyze the gap between our expectations and the JBOR data actually received, in both quantitative and qualitative senses.

As discussed earlier, GAL 1353 *required* State Employment Security Agencies in states implementing Job Banks in Fiscal Year 1970 to provide JBOR data beginning in February 1970 and continuing for one full year after implementation. In addition, as discussed earlier, we visited several state agencies and obtained informal assurances that data would be provided before GAL 1353 became effective, i.e., February 1970. In general these informal "gentlemen's agreements" yielded poor results. Of the first six Job Banks implemented, only two furnished JBOR data on approximately the schedule agreed upon. In addition to the shortfall in the *quantity* of JBOR data received, there were *quality* shortcomings as well. The methods we used to detect and deal with these are described in the subsection, "Cleaning up the Data," p. 81.

Although our analysis is somewhat speculative, several reasons may be advanced to help explain the failure of many states to provide JBOR data as expected.

First, it should be pointed out that JBOR was an ambitious undertaking. It was a more comprehensive data-gathering system than had ever before been implemented in the Employment Service. It was the first computerized data-gathering system implemented in the Employment Service. It was implemented on relatively short notice, at a time when state agency research, operating, and data-processing staffs were under great pressure to introduce other automated reporting systems (ESARS and Cost Accounting). All of these problems were beyond the control of these researchers.

A second issue, more difficult to evaluate, concerns the organizational way in which JBOR was implemented. Its designers and major advocates were all outsiders, in the sense of being outside the organizations officially responsible for producing data from operating systems. The assistant secretary was an academic, "in town" for what was sure to be a short tour of duty. These researchers were known short-timers. LLA was understood by us to have had various conflicts, in connection with the initial formation of DMMS and assignment of responsibility for computer-assisted man-job matching systems, with some of those who were ordinarily responsible for data-gathering.

We do not know the importance of this organizational factor, although we think in retrospect it may have been very important. As noted earlier, our experience with the ICESA R&R Committee suggested such problems.[4] Further, OMMDS was somewhat less aggressive in pursuing delinquent states than these researchers had expected them to be, although this may have been a simple misunderstanding.

The third reason may be that we were simply naive as to the degree to which state agencies respond to federal reporting requirements. Although data on this matter are not available to us, we understand from informal discussion that compliance with reporting requirements is frequently less than perfect. A former assistant secretary of labor for manpower explained why states are not always cooperative.

The Wagner-Peyser Act which has provided the legislative base for the employment service system for thirty-seven years is inadequate in at least three important respects. . . .

Second, the fact that total withdrawal of financial support to a state is the only sanction available to the federal government makes enforcement of standards of performance impossible. No federal administrator could, or would want to risk shutting down the entire state employment security system. To even suggest this kind of action is sheer fantasy.[5]

Establishing Comparison Data:
The Comparison Cities

In order to determine what difference Job Banks make, we thought it necessary to have some basis for comparison, i.e., some base group that serves the function of a control group. To some extent, each Job Bank provides its own "control" through the comparison of pre- and post-Job Bank performance. However, such a pre- and post-comparison assumes that conditions in the two periods were identical, with presence or absence of Job Bank being the only variable. Clearly this assumption is not tenable, because of variations in labor-market conditions, Employment Service program emphases, and other variables.[6] A change in the unemployment rate is perhaps the most obvious example of a factor that could make simple pre- vs. post-comparison invalid: i.e., given a shift in unemployment rate, is it Job Bank or the changed labor-market environment that brought about the observed change in Employment Service.

To overcome problems such as that spelled out above, researchers commonly include a control consisting of an outside comparison group. In the Job Bank case, this would ideally be a set of cities just like those in which Job Banks were installed, except that they would not have Job Banks. By making before and after implementation comparison between the Job Bank cities and these non-Job Bank control cities, all effects other than Job Bank would hopefully be held constant.

It is well-known that social science researchers are typically unable to establish ideal comparison groups. Cain and Hollister note that "randomization [of treatment in social programs] is seldom attempted for reasons having to do with attitudes of the administrators of a program, local pressures from the client population, or various logistic problems. Indeed, all these reasons may serve to botch an *attempted* randomization procedure. Furthermore, we can say with greater certitude that the ideal 'double-blind experiment with placebos' is almost impossible to achieve."[7]

The Job Bank experience provides insight into the difficulty of achieving a satisfactory experimental design, insofar as including a control group is concerned, in evaluating a social action program. Clearly, the Job Bank cities were not chosen as a random sample of the cities in the United States. Rather, by specific directive of the secretary of labor (March 19, 1969 memorandum for the president), they were the larger cities. Further, Job Banks tended to be located in the states whose Employment Services were more cooperative with the National Office than agencies in other states. (For example, California was designated by USTES to implement six Job Banks in fiscal year 1970 on a basis of city size. However, the California agency chose to implement only one Job Bank in this period.)

Initially, in designing this research, the investigators were mindful of the desirability of obtaining a control group composed of non-Job Bank cities with characteristics identical to those of the Job Bank cities. However, we did not argue for such a matched sample for three reasons. First, agency policy was to install Job Banks in at least fifty-six cities, including the forty largest cities in the nation, by a certain date. Achievement of this goal had highest priority. Thus we knew it would not be possible to have ideal controls for the largest cities, because of the policy of having Job Banks in each of the forty largest cities.

Our second reason for not pushing for control cities was the expense and difficulty involved in obtaining the data. For a variety of reasons, there was widespread resistance through the agency, at both the federal and state levels, to imposing the heavy reporting burden associated with collecting data for control cities. We were philosophically aligned with this view to some degree, and we had previously agreed with LLA—in order to obtain his more enthusiastic support and because it seemed reasonable from larger organizational point of view—to collect no data except that needed for operating purposes. (It will be recalled that all of the JBOR input was data needed for operations and that the output was developed at very low cost through a set of programs included in the National Office Standard Computer Program Package used by most Job Banks).

Finally, we expected that our anticipated large sample size of over forty cities would allow us to reduce the danger of labor-market changes obscuring the impact of the Job Bank Program. We hoped, short of general recession, to be able to control for changes in labor-market environment either by comparing changes in our evaluative criteria for stable labor-market cities and changing labor-market cities or by adjusting the performance data with statistically derived correction factors.

Even though we did not raise the question of setting up ideal control cities for the reasons discussed above, the issue was eventually given thorough consideration. At about the time GAL 1353, requiring Job Bank cities to produce JBOR data, became effective, ASM (1) raised the control city issue himself. ASM (1) had an academic background and was very favorably disposed toward program research.

On February 2, a memo was sent to ASM(1) stating our belief that JBOR data should not be collected from control cities, for the reasons given above. On February 10, ASM (1) replied that he wanted control city data, despite these arguments, and that steps should be taken to collect such data. During the next several weeks work went forward on plans to collect JBOR data from twelve control cities that had been paired with twelve of the smaller Job Bank cities. The pairing was based on comparability of population, unemployment rate, and industry structure.

In early April, ASM (1) issued instructions to expand Job Banks to cities of a quarter-million population that could be operational by June 30 and were not covered within the original fifty-six-city goal. Steps were immediately taken to implement this instruction; specifically, the state agencies were asked to nominate additional Job Bank cities. Among the cities nominated by the states for immediate Job Bank implementation were five of the twelve tentatively designated control cities.

LLA was thus presented with a dilemma: should he work to see that as many Job Banks as possible were implemented by June 30 (his primary assignment), or should he perhaps sacrifice this goal to a degree in order to protect the integrity of the control city set? (The next-best potential control cities were not nearly as well-matched with the comparable Job Banks as were the original set.)

Actually, this situation was not viewed initially as a dilemma in the Job Bank Division. When we first raised the matter, LLA and his principal aide said, in effect, "oh, we're sure that the assistant secretary wants us to go ahead implementing as fast as possible, even if it means no control cities." We responded that this appeared to us to be an example of a saying we had heard about governmental decision-making: "clerks make the decisions the division chiefs should make, and division chiefs make the decisions that the assistant secretaries should make." The implication of our statement was obviously that LLA should ask ASM (1) for a clarification, given the conflict in instructions.

LLA agreed that he was not 100 percent certain that ASM (1) really wanted the control cities sacrificed, and instructed one of the present authors to draft a memo to ASM (1) pointing out the conflict in orders. The memo originally drafted pointed out the conflict, suggested that a possible compromise would be to conduct a retrospective study using as controls, cities that were slow implementing Job Banks, and asking for further instructions.

Communications originating in the Job Bank Division went through three layers of management above the division before reaching the ASM (1). Each of these higher levels may approve, alter, or stop any upward-bound communications. In the case of the memo under discussion, the paragraph asking for instructions was deleted from the memo at some higher level in the agency, and was replaced by a different paragraph. The replacement paragraph changed the memo from a request for clarification to a statement of intent. Of course, this type of distortion is not unique to the Department of Labor. A close student of bureaucratic organizations has observed that "when information must be passed through many officials each of whom condenses it somewhat before passing it on to the next, the final output will be very different in quality from the original input; that is, significant distortions will occur.[8]

In the case at hand, LLA explained that the change had been made by his superiors because the manpower administrator "doesn't say to ASM (1): tell me what to do! Rather, he says what he is doing and lets the (ASM (1)) disagree if he wants. If the manpower administrator signed the memo, that's an order to go ahead with implementation."

ASM (1) did not respond to this memo, so implementation was given priority over establishment of control cities.

On May 11, the chief of the office charged with collecting JBOR data from both Job Bank and control cities (OMMDS) wrote to the LLA (actually to LLA's superiors, as required by operating procedures) noting that several cities initially nominated as Job Bank control cities were likely to become Job Banks in the near future. This memo asked for instructions as to how to proceed.

On May 19, LLA replied to OMMDS, agreeing that seven of the twelve cities originally designated controls would in all likelihood become Job Bank cities in the near future. LLA then listed seven substitute cities that were unlikely to become Job Bank cities in the near future, and asked that JBOR-type data be collected from these seven cities, and from five of the twelve originally designated control cities. This memo asked that the data collection process begin on July 1.

Development of a field memorandum providing instructions for collection and submittal of JBOR by the new set of control cities continued through the rest of May and into June. In mid-June, however, the chief of OISO—the office within OMMDS responsible for collecting JBOR data—whose staff were developing the field memorandum, remained unconvinced of the desirability of collecting control city JBOR data. His concern stemmed from several factors, including his belief that the newly designated cities were not well-matched with their Job Bank mates, as well as several procedural questions.

At this point (mid-June) the present authors were approaching the end of their tours in the agency and were working to finish various tasks, including finalizing procedures for gathering the JBOR data from control cities. However, the Field Memorandum had not gone out by June 30, when we left the agency.

On July 3, ASM (1) was appointed associate director of a different agency, and the former manpower administrator was named Assistant Secretary. At this point, work stopped on the field memorandum requiring designated control cities to collect JBOR data.

This story casts light on the decision-making process in a large agency, as well as explaining why plans to collect JBOR data from a set of control cities went awry. The effort to obtain rigorous control data had strong backing: ASM (1) specifically ordered the development of such data, and technicians (the present authors) were available who had the knowledge, time, desire, and organizational positions needed to push for implementation of the ASM (1)'s directive. Despite these exceptionally favorable circumstances, control city plans were delayed, altered, delayed further, and finally dropped. It is little wonder that ideal control data are not collected in other less propitious but more typical circumstances.

The consequence of these events was that we did not have "control" cities in the scientifically accepted sense of the word, but rather we had to settle for "comparison" cities. This circumstance caused several difficulties in interpreting the data, as will be discussed in the next section.

Analyzing the Data and
Drawing Conclusions

Cleaning Up the Data. While aiding in the implementation of Job Banks and JBOR, we became particularly aware of the problems associated with the start-up of these two systems and recognized that some of the JBOR data would probably be in error. To minimize the effect of this on our analysis, we visually checked all incoming JBOR data before keypunching it. When apparently erroneous data were received (data that fell outside of limits obtained through discussions with knowledgeable Department of Labor personnel), we had the National Office ask the particular job bank for an explanation. Since a reply to such an inquiry is mandatory, we almost invariably got a reply. Its form was either corrected data, an explanation of the apparent deviant values, or an admission that the data were wrong but that the correct data were unavailable. In the last case, we eliminated the corresponding data from our analysis.

The data-editing system described above was useful but insufficient. We became particularly aware of this when we ran some multiple regression analysis and got some unbelievable results, which when examined closely were found to be the result of incorrect data. For example, one city had more regular placements than it had applicants. In two others, the 1970 activity levels were found to be incredibly smaller in value than the 1971 data. Phone calls in the first case resulted in finding and correcting the error, thus providing us usable data. In the second case, we learned that only a small fraction of the actual 1970 activities had been reported due to start-up problems. Since this type of error could not be corrected, these two cities had to be deleted for the months in question.

In order to overcome the problem of unidentified incorrect data, we performed an "outlier analysis," i.e., whenever one of our computer-performed regression analyses was run, we obtained a printout of the residual errors, the deviations between the values predicted by the regression model and the actual data values. When a residual error was found that could occur by chance alone less than one time in twenty, we investigated by phoning or writing the corresponding Job Bank and determined if it were caused by incorrect data. In the case where we were able to obtain corrected data, we used it. If the data were irretrievably incorrect, we eliminated them from the analysis. In the case of small data bases such as ours, this approach to cleaning up the data is useful and often necessary but can be abused if any bias is allowed to determine which data are to be examined. We provided safeguards in this respect. For example, the effect on the hypothesis of eliminating the data was not determined, much less used, and the only data that were eliminated were those where an actual reporting error could be identified. In essence, we followed the standards adhered to when this statistical technique is applied to the design of statistical quality control charts, as it often is.[9] As a result of the visual check and outlier analysis, the data used in the statistical analysis were relatively error-free.

It should be noted that some of the performance data for the Job Bank cities were obtained in a different manner than were the data for the comparison cities. This can be seen by examining the part of Appendix 2 having to do with goal achievement. The data taken from Table VII of JBOR were obtained by the Job Banks either by hand tally or by using the ADP system, ESARS, and were obtained by the comparison cities using these same methods. However, the data taken from Table I of JBOR were obtained by the Job Banks using computer programs that automatically recorded the activities of the (computerized) Job Bank, but were obtained by the comparison cities either with hand tallies or ESARS. Thus the data relating to some performance measures were not strictly comparable between the two groups.

There was no way of ascertaining the exact effect of this on our results. We think that it was small. For instance, while one recording system may be biased either high or low, for all measures we took before-and-after differences, thus subtracting out some of the possible systematic biases. Others were caught with the outlier analysis. It is still possible, of course, that there were some undetected, hopefully small, effects on our results. These would tend not to have much of an impact on our conclusions in that they would incline to result in Type I errors (accepting differences in performance that were not really there), but we found no differences to begin with. For an effect of different data collection systems to result in an incorrect conclusion, the effect would: (1) have not to be neutralized through year-to-year subtraction; (2) have not to be caught in the data cleanup procedure; (3) have to be of a magnitude almost equal to that of a legitimate performance difference and in the same direction; and (4) have to affect the majority of the measures used to evaluate achievement of the particular goal about which the conclusion was drawn. This series of events is extremely unlikely.

Measuring Performance and Coping with Nonequivalence

The first requirement of evaluation research is the determination of efficacy. Evaluation research efforts must, therefore, seek to approximate the experimental model as much as possible—we do not do so often enough and some of the so-called evaluation designs of the current mass programs have completely foregone an experimental or quasi-experimental approach. Admittedly, there is a limit to the extent controlled experiments can be conducted within these programs. Nevertheless it is possible in most instances to make use of at least rudimentary or quasi-designs to approximate the conditions of the before-after and/or pre-post test designs, be it through randomization or statistical procedures.[10]

Our design is called by Campbell and Stanley a quasi-experimental design, one without full control over the scheduling and allocation of experimental stimuli.[11] More specifically, it is labeled the "nonequivalent control group design." It involves the comparison of performance changes in the Job Bank cities with performance changes in comparison cities.[12] As will be discussed in the next section, for some additional measures not reported by the comparison cities, Job Bank performance changes relatively independent of minor economic changes were tested against the null hypothesis.

As noted, we used eighteen Job Bank cities and twelve comparison cities in our analyses of goal achievement. Three kinds of analyses were run, each yielding essentially the same results with respect to the effects of Job Banks. One, involving the use of simple linear regression, consisted of regressing the particular performance measure on the binary variable (presence vs. absence of Job Bank). After determining that the population and 1970 unemployment levels of the Job Banks were statistically and significantly different from those of the comparison cities, we ran the second type of analysis involving the use of stepwise multiple regression.[13] We regressed the performance measures on population, 1970 unemployment, and the binary variable.

The third type of analysis was similar to the first, but was run after deleting the four Job Bank cities with populations greater than that of the largest comparison city and deleting the two comparison cities that were smaller than the smallest Job Bank cities. The mean population of the resulting two groups were almost identical. The raw data for these analyses appears in Table 1-A.

A statistician might wonder why we bothered with the first and third analyses. The answer is that we were attempting to provide understandable answers to the administrators when they asked us how we arrived at this or that result or conclusion. Our first and third analyses were equivalent to using a t-test, and discussions concerning "two columns of data" and "the average Job Bank performance was . . . " proved fruitful. On the other hand, discussions concerning stepwise multiple regression would have involved either long and tedious explanations or a lot of handwaving and appeals for faith. We thought that neither of these would be very acceptable to practical-minded administrators. In discussing the obstacles to implementation of research findings, Shulberg and Baker note the frequent and disastrous occurrence where "the administrator alleges that the researcher's findings have been presented in an unnecessarily frustrating and abstract manner.[14] We feel that one of the reasons

Table 1-A
Population and Unemployment of Job Bank and Comparison Cities

Job Bank	SMSA Population (000)	February 1970 Unemployment (%)	March 1970 Unemployment (%)	Comparison City	SMSA Population (000)	February 1970 Unemployment (%)	March 1970 Unemployment (%)
Albuquerque	316	4.5	4.3	Akron	679	3.3	3.4
Birmingham	739	3.3	3.3	Davenport	363	4.5	4.3
Buffalo	1,349	4.8	4.6	Duluth	265	6.0	5.7
Cincinnati	1,385	3.7	3.4	Gary	633	3.5	3.3
Cleveland	2,064	3.0	2.9	Knoxville	400	3.0	3.1
Columbia	323	3.1	2.9	Sacramento	801	6.9	6.5
Columbus	916	3.0	3.0	Shreveport	294	4.2	4.1
Des Moines	286	2.5	2.5	South Bend	280	5.2	5.0
Hartford	664	3.6	3.5	Tampa	1,013	2.4	2.3
Little Rock	323	2.8	2.5	Trenton	304	3.9	3.8
Memphis	770	3.2	3.0	Worcester	344	4.4	4.3
Minneapolis	1,814	2.5	2.6	Youngstown	536	3.9	4.2
Oklahoma City	641	2.8	3.0				
Omaha	541	3.0	3.1				
Phoenix	968	3.2	3.1				
Syracuse	636	4.4	4.5				
Tulsa	476	3.6	3.8				
Wichita	389	5.9	6.7				

that we were able to get some of our findings acted upon was that we consciously avoided this problem to the extent we could do so.

As noted earlier, and not too surprisingly, the three kinds of analyses in the study yielded essentially the same results.

Drawing Conclusions.[15] As noted earlier, we compared changes in Job Bank performance against changes in comparison city performance where comparison city data were obtainable and against the hypothesis of no change where comparison city data were not obtainable. The results of these comparisons, are shown in Appendix 2. All results were reported, i.e., no a priori levels of significance were used to screen results for feedback purposes with regard to goal achievement.

In order to draw conclusions concerning the achievement of the individual labor-market-related goals, we studied the results concerning those performance measures that were related to the goal in question. Our reasoning concerning the relative achievement of each goal is detailed in Chapter 3, under the subheading, "Findings Concerning Program Goals."

Strictly speaking, our findings concerning goal achievement apply only to these eighteen Job Banks. The differences between these and the other Job Banks are as follows: (1) as noted earlier, the less cooperative state agencies either did not implement Job Banks or implemented them so late that they were not among our eighteen; (2) the state agencies were asked to nominate candidate cities for Job Bank implementation, presumably nominating those whose management would be most receptive to the idea and most competent and therefore probably able to implement quickly; (3) the more cooperative and effective agencies got the JBOR system implemented, a prerequisite for inclusion in our data base. As a consequence we belive that, statistical measures aside, if the Job Banks that we studied are different from other Job Banks or from the comparison cities, they are different in that they are more cooperative with the National Office.[16]

There are, of course, other possible differences between our Job Banks and other Job Banks. Most of these differences would not have a significant effect on performance. One difference that might have an effect would be a difference between the degree to which our Job Banks approached optimal design and the degree to which the other Job Banks did. We tested for this using the data in Tables 1-B and 1-C. Table 1-B contains data on the design variables of the other Job Bank cities and is comparable to the data in Appendix 2 of this report concerning the design variables in our Job Bank cities. Table 1-C shows the summary statistics comparing the two groups and the statistical significance of the differences. We conclude that the two groups are sufficiently similar in their design variables that we can generalize our conclusions from the Job Banks that we studied to all the Job Banks operating in the same time interval.

Table 1-B
Design Variables in Job Banks not Subjected to Statistical Analysis

City	Order Taking Spec.	Order Taking N.S.	Referral Spec.	Referral N.S.	Continuous Err's	CAs 0-2	CAs 3+	Books/Int. C1	Books/Int. 1+	Number of ES Offices	Referrals Verified by Interviewers	Referrals Verified by Phone by Central Unit
1. Atlanta	X		X		.105	X		X		4	.01	.00
2. Baltimore		X	X		.042		X	X		6	.01	.00
3. Boston		X	X		.000		X		X	19	.00	.40
4. Bridgeport	X		X		X	.023	X		X		2	.00	.60
5. Charleston	N/A		N/A		.028	N/A		X		2	.65	.00
6. Chicago	X		N/A		.108	X		X		22	N/A	N/A
7. Denver	N/A		X		.000	X		X		4	N/A	N/A
8. Detroit	X		X		.051	X		X		4	.55	.00
9. Greensboro		X	N/A		.048	X			X	6	.02	.20
10. Kansas City (two forms; different answers)	X		X		.044		X		X	7	N/A	N/A
11. Newark		X	X		.039	X		X		6	.05	.95
12. New Haven	X		X		.000	X		X		N/A	.05	.80
13. Paterson		X		X	.090	X			X	3	.02	.98
14. Philadelphia		X		X	.159		X	X		10	.005	.21
15. Pittsburgh		X		X	.196		X	X		8	.005	.38
16. Portland	N/A		X		.106		X		X	15	.45	.00
17. San Antonio		X	X		.109		X		X	6	.675	.00
18. San Diego		X	N/A		.000		X		X	5	.85	.00
19. Seattle		X		X	.000	N/A			X	45	.99	.00
20. St. Louis	X		X		.098	X			X	14	.25	.75
21. Wilmington	N/A		X		.033		X		X	5	.70	.00

Table 1-C
Summary Comparison of the Two Groups of Job Banks

Design Variable	State of Interest	JB Cities Statistic	Other Cities Statistic	Difference	Sig. Level[a]
1. Order-taking	% SPEC	.294	.412	−.118	.50
2. Referrals	% SPEC	.875	.722	.153	.30
3. Cont. err's	X	.081	.061	.202	.30
4. Comm. agencies	% 3+	.722	.474	.248	.15
5. Books/int.	% 1+	.444	.476	−.032	N.S.
6. E.S. offices	At/Above Median	.471	.700	−.229	.30
7. Int. ver. ref's	X	.263	.294	−.031	N.S.
8. Cent. ver. ref's	X	.320	.243	.027	N.S.

[a]Two-tailed t-tests.

Determining Optimal Job Bank Design Configuration

We undertook the task of determining the optimum organization design because it seemed that a "pass-fail" analysis of the Job Banks would be insufficient. For a variety of reasons, it is frequently reasonable to make marginal improvements in existing public policy programs rather than to discontinue them and leave some goal still unfulfilled. The question, of course, is "exactly what are the improvements?"

Determining optimal organization design is a problem that has been explored by practitioners and behavioral scientists for a long time. The resulting principles or theories are frequently contradictory or in need of qualification based on the organization's environment, traditions, or personnel. It appears that a rigorous empirical approach would be useful in those situations where it is possible. We found that it was possible to use this approach for determining optimum "levels" of the design variables of the Job Banks.

The approach involved three steps. The first step was to identify the key design variables. We accomplished this through discussions with knowledgeable people in the Department of Labor and by designing and conducting an interview study in the four SMSAs where Job Banks had been in operation for the longest period. The study involved semistructured interviews with Job Bank managers, Employment Service interviewers, and local employers.

The second step was to obtain information on the levels of these variables as they existed in the various job banks. There was in fact considerable variation among the Job Banks in the design profile that they manifested. We obtained this information with a questionnaire, which was completed for each job bank by a person familiar with its design and operation. The completion of this questionnaire was voluntary, and many cities went unreported. The effect of the consequent reduction on our data base is noted in the section, "Obtaining Design Data," p. 106.

The third step was to determine the effect of these variables, shown in Table 2-3, on the performance measures of Table 2-2. Only the particular design variables that seemed most critical and subject to change (if they were found to be at a less effective level) were included in our analysis. The particular levels of these variables that were related to highest performance were to be identified as optimal levels and recommended for universal adoption among the Job Banks, unless there was some interactive effect with other variables that would preclude such adoption. The details of the statistical analysis used in determining the optimal design configuration are described in the section "Analyzing the Data and Drawing Conclusions."

Obtaining Information from Job Bank
Users and Clients: The Interview Studies

Report on Job Bank Interview Study. The purpose of the study was to gather data on aspects of Job Bank operation not covered by the Job Bank Operations Review. Specifically, the study was aimed at determining the impact of Job Bank on the operation of local Community Agencies, employers, and the work routines of Employment Service Staff.

The study was conducted during January, February, and March 1970 in Baltimore, Portland, St. Louis, and Seattle. Twenty employers, half selected as good customers of the Employment Service and half chosen randomly, were interviewed. At least twelve placement interviewers and counselors and four or five Community Agencies were interviewed in each city.

The authors designed and supervised the study and conducted many of the interviews. Most of the employer and Community Agency interviews in Portland and Seattle were conducted by Professor Eaton Conant of the University of Oregon. Professor E.E. Liebhafsky of the University of Missouri interviewed most of the sample employers and Community Agencies in St. Louis.

Study of Community Agency Participation in Job Banks in Four Cities. During February and March 1970, Office of Systems Support staff and consultants interviewed Employment Service (ES) management and a sample of Community Agencies in Baltimore, St. Louis, Portland, and Seattle. The purpose of the study was to learn more about the role of CAs in Job Banks and to gather ideas for increasing the effectiveness of ES-CA relations in Job Bank cities.

A total of eighteen CAs were interviewed. Officials of the public schools, Division of Vocational Rehabilitation, and Urban League were interviewed in each city. The other respondents were primarily miscellaneous community action agencies.

The number of agencies interviewed and the number of agencies participating in the various Job Banks follow:

	Number of CAs Interviewed	Number of CAs in Job Bank
Baltimore	5	18
St. Louis	4	2
Portland	5	7
Seattle	4	0

Scope and Organization of CA Operations

1. In each city, Vocational Rehabilitation and Urban League have been in the job placement field for many years. In general, the other organizations interviewed have only been in the placement field for two to five years.
2. None of the CAs approached the ES in placement volume, although several organizations do a substantial volume. The range of annual placement volumes in the various cities, by class of agency is shown below.

Public Schools	1500-5000
Voc. Rehab	1000-2000
Urban League	350-1400
Misc. Agencies	200-1700

3. Nearly all CAs studied have an inventory of job openings. However, most openings are job developed for individuals, so the openings inventories tend to be small.
4. Job placement is not a central function of any CA in the sample. All the agencies have a case orientation toward their clientele, and placement is just one of many services provided.

Organization of CA Involvement in Job Banks

1. No CAs are yet involved in the Seattle Job Bank, although negotiations concerning participation are underway. In St. Louis and Portland, the CAs have Job Bank openings lists on their own premises, in contrast to Baltimore where CAs must use the lists on ES premises. Employer names and addresses are included on the list in all cities.
2. Maryland and Missouri do not require CAs to list their own job openings in Job Bank, but ES policy in Oregon and Washington is to require such listing as a condition of participation.
3. In all cities, there is some ES-CA interaction in CEPs or Multi-Service Centers. The ES people generally operate as the placement arm of these joint efforts.

Scope and Effectiveness of CA Participation in Job Banks

1. CAs have not made a large number of placements in Job Bank jobs in any city. In Baltimore, about one-half of 1 percent of Job Bank placements are by CAs, and in the other cities the CA proportion of total placements is even less.
2. Virtually no CA openings are being put in the Job Bank in any city. Oregon has not enforced its policy of forced listing, and the listing requirement policy has been a barrier to CA participation in Seattle.
3. There is some evidence that CAs have a greater tendency to make poor referrals than do ES placement personnel. (a) CAs in Portland made 108 referrals, but only three placements in December 1970. (b) Some ES personnel suggested that overreferral and poor referral within JB was due to CAs fouling up. (c) A CA director said "community workers should not do job referral, as that wasn't their bag. Let the ES people do that."

CA Views of Job Bank

1. In general, the CAs believe the Job Bank concept is good.
2. All CAs oppose having to list all openings, because so many are job developed or provided by employers with a special interest in helping a particular group such as ex-prisoners. However, most CAs would be willing to list some openings.
3. Baltimore CAs said they would use Job Bank more if they could have the lists on their own premises. CAs in other cities said having to go to the ES to use the lists would inhibit their participation.
4. Four of the thirteen CAs with access to Job Bank lists said the lists contain openings suitable for their clients, and three additional agencies said the lists contained *some* suitable openings. However, four agencies said Job Bank did not contain suitable openings. Further, eight agencies said their clients were seldom successful in getting jobs from these listings, and only two (DVR and Prisoners Aid in Baltimore) reported that their applicants were usually successful in getting jobs from Job Bank listings. The belief that Job Bank openings are not suitable, and that CA clients seldom succeed in getting jobs by the Job Bank route is almost invariably attributed by CAs to their applicants' inability to compete with more advantaged applicants.
5. Ten CAs expressed the opinion that the local ES had an adequate number of outreach stations, and that they were properly located. However, two of these respondents added the gratuitous comment that "it's their [ES] attitude, not their location, that's the problem." Six CAs, mostly social agencies operating in the ghetto on a decentralized basis, felt that the ES does not have enough outreach stations. Overall, those CAs which themselves operate in a centralized mode believed the ES had enough offices, whereas the decentralized and/or ghetto-located CAs believed the contrary.

6. The CAs interviewed were remarkably consistent in both the scope and intensity of their criticism of the ES. To some degree, their views of JB could not be disentangled from their general attitude toward the ES. The images of the ES and the preferred model are listed below.

ES is	ES should be
Oriented toward placement transactions	Case-oriented (give interviewer sensitivity training)
Too centralized	Decentralized to where the people are
Too bureaucratic	Service oriented: reduce the red tape

Summary of Employer Interview Responses

1. Two-thirds of the employers had personal or telephone contact with the ES at least once a month, and most of the rest spoke with the ES several times a year. Thus we interviewed mostly employers who were frequent ES users and had information on which to base their responses.
2. Employers were generally satisfied with promptness of referrals, and one-third perceive improvement since job bank. A few employers were very laudatory about improvement in this regard, and had increased use of the Employment Service as a result.
3. Overall, employer responses indicated no significant shift in level of use of the Employment Service. Most employers said they used the ES the same amount as before Job Bank, and the slightly larger number of "less" than "more" responses was accounted for by Seattle employers doing less hiring because of the decline in business activity in that area.
4. Although three-fifths of the employers contacted know about Job Bank, a significant number had not heard about it. In Seattle, where Job Bank had been in operation only four or five months, three-fourths of the employers contacted did not mention Job Bank.
5. Most employers reported no change in frequency of ES contact for referrals or for solicitation by the ES in the period since Job Bank was started. However, eleven employers perceived a decline in industrial service contacts, whereas only three said there had been an increase in such contacts.
6. Nearly half of the employers in the sample report an increase in the number of contacts with other CAs in the past year. However, few commented unfavorably on this change.
7. A great deal of criticism of certain aspects of Job Bank emerged from the interviews. This criticism seems especially significant for two reasons. First, Job Bank was not mentioned at any time by the interviewer. Second, the

question which elicited these comments was phrased "Please suggest some ways the ES could improve its service to your organization."

In three of the four cities studied, placement interviewers are all generalists, whereas in Portland interviewers specialize although they do some referral outside their specialties. Eleven of the thirty ES sample employers and eight of the thirty random sample employers specifically complained about the change from specialized to generalist order-taking or placement interviewers. As the following quotes show, the strength of feeling varied widely, but the gist of the complaint is that referral quality drops.

On the other hand, only two ES sample and no random sample employers in Portland complained about referral quality and in these two complaining cases Job Bank was not singled out as the villain.

These results parallel and confirm the findings of the Six-City Study.

Five employers complained about overreferral and a few said the verification card was an inconvenience. Interestingly, none of the employers who mentioned overreferral realized the role of the verification card in this regard.

A few employers praised the ES when asked how service could be improved, and several miscellaneous comments and criticisms were given. However, the bulk of the comments related to the match accomplished in the Job Bank or to other Job Bank factors.

Specific Comments

Seattle
1. ES sample (N = 10)
   a. A heavy ES user[a] retailer: "ES needs specialists for particular industries. Can't get properly screened applicants any more."
   b. "Would like same ES person to handle all his orders. Wants same person that takes order to do all referrals because he knows my requirements. They just sent anyone out, no longer sending qualified people."
   c. Restaurant association manager: "Specialization of placement very important in restaurant industry. Our members say since specialization stopped, they are getting much poorer referrals, and complaining to him about this."
   d. Convalescent center—heavy user: "We would rather deal with one person. Too often we get different people handling different orders. ES doesn't really check out job applicants they sent us."
   e. Large[b] mail order house—light user: "We tell ES what we are looking for, but what shows up is not the same. There is a communications breakdown between us and the ES. We thing ES made tactical error in curtailing

---

[a]Defined as at least 30 percent of new hires in at least one broad occupational group.
[b]Over 1000 employees.

service and procedures which has shut out the more qualified applicants."

2. Random Sample (N = 10) but five haven't hired through ES in past three years)

   a. Large[b] bank—light user: "Would prefer dealing with one person, so we could get more qualified applicants and more what we ask for. They aren't really trying to send qualified people."

   b. Department store—light user: "ES people need to better understand the kind of person and occupational experience we need."

   c. Manufacturer—light user: "ES should go back to specialization. Also should call to describe applicants before sending them."

Portland

1. ES Sample (N = 10)

   a. Manufacturing company—heavy user: "We give orders. Somewhere communications gets mixed up, and we don't get people we want. Also, we never deal with same person, so we can't follow up a request."

   b. Hotel—heavy user: "Too many referrals. They are working to get colored people in, and this is part of it. Referral slip system is a pain in the neck. They've changed for three times this year. They should simplify the form. Overall they do a good job, but interviewers who don't know our needs don't screen adequately."

   c. Utility—heavy user: "Sometimes I mail verification card, then get call asking about the same referral."

   d. Manufacturing firm—light user: "Need better pre-screening. I ask for journeyman carpenter or certified welder, and just get completely unqualified people. Also they overrefer, and the verification cards are a pain. Why do I have to do that?"

2. Random sample (N = 10, but two haven't hired through ES in past three years) No negative comments related to job bank or recent organizational changes.

St. Louis

1. ES sample (N = 10)

   a. Restaurant chain—heavy user: "Regionalize Job Bank to show distance to jobs. Should be possible to contact particular office on specific needs."

   b. General office of manufacturing company—heavy user: "Since Job Bank, we've been getting less selective referrals."

   c. Manufacturing firm—heavy user: "ES should have one or two people who work directly with one or two employer people. Personal contact has been reduced since installation of the computer. We knew the people at the St. Ann office. Now we call the Central Job Bank and lose the personal touch."

---

[b]Over 1000 employees.

    d. Manufacturing company—heavy user: "The new order department, putting orders on teletype, slows down referral of applicants and too many workers apply to our plant."

    e. Department store—heavy user: "Putting job orders on a computer system causes the ES to lose the personal touch of the local office."

    f. Drug store chain—heavy user: "It would help for ES to show job filled when they are filled. Applicants keep coming after jobs are filled."

    g. Manufacturing firm—heavy user: "Return to using old referral cards. New forms are added expense and aggravation because we must look in files for information when the cards arrive."

2. Random (N = 10)

Manufacturing firm—light user: "Would like to see the personalized approach again, dealing with one source. In the past, very pleased with ES, but no longer my ace in the hole. Now that jobs are on computer, it takes a week to get referrals rather than a day."

(Most employers in this group used ES very little.)

Baltimore

1. ES sample (N = 10)

    a. Large manufacturer—formerly heavy, now light user: "Go back to specialist set-up. You can't educate the whole damned ES to what I mean by a machinist or a shipyard fitter, but you can educate a few specialists."

    b. Manufacturer—heavy user: "It used to be a little more personalized, and we got better service. When we place an order now, we have to explain the job more. They used to know this automatically."

    c. Insurance company—light user: "They keep sending people a week after the order has been cancelled. Quality of referrals is worse than it used to be."

    d. Manufacturer—light user: "We can't get orders cancelled. They keep sending people."

    e. Hospital—light user: "They won't follow the specifications we give them. I even went to talk with them to explain our needs, and it didn't help so I've stopped using them."

    f. Manufacturer—light user: "Job Bank has impaired their efficiency. We get four or five people calling to refer now, instead of one. This is a real nuisance, because it ends up with overreferral. They don't screen or pay any attention to stated qualifications. This has gotten much worse since Job Bank. I even gave a talk to all their interviewers, and it hasn't helped."

Summary of ES Staff Interviews. Interviews were conducted in each city with six to eight employment interviewers, two to three counselors, and one VER. All of those interviewed had been in their jobs since before the local Job Bank started.

1. Half of those interviewed felt they had more paper work under the Job Bank operation than formerly. However, in Baltimore, which was the only city that had a Job Bank longer than eight months at the time of the study, the consensus was that Job Bank had slightly reduced the amount of paper work, if it had any effect. This suggests that the change in the system, rather than the nature of the new system, may have led people to perceive that Job Bank caused more paper work. This hypothesis could be tested by repeating the interviews a year hence.

2. Three-fifths of the ES staff believed the disadvantaged were served better by the Job Bank system than by the previous system, and only one-fifth felt disadvantaged applicants were less well served. To some extent, respondents simply said they knew Job Bank was better because the statistics proved it. However, several staff pointed out that Job Bank offered a broader selection of jobs and clues to where to do job development.

   Most interviewers who believe Job Bank has hurt the cause of serving the disadvantaged explain by saying that placing such people depends on close relations with employers, which Job Bank (in its generalist mode) destroys. An articulate quote: "We're gradually losing contact with employers, and loss of rapport makes it *harder* to place a disadvantaged applicant. You lose the clout that's implicit in a close personal relationship."

3. Only two-fifths of the staff believe Job Bank leads to better service for the nondisadvantaged applicant, although an additional two-fifths say it has had no effect in this regard.

   Most of those who believe Job Bank helps the nondisadvantaged cite the broad exposure of openings. Interestingly, a significant number of those who say Job Bank has no effect on this group added that agency policy was reducing service to the nondisadvantaged but that Job Bank had no role in this.

   Frequently, those who said Job Bank hurts service to the nondisadvantaged were really saying that agency policy on whom to serve was changing.

4. Half of the ES respondents said employers are served less well under Job Bank than formerly, whereas one-fourth felt they are served better. Reasons for the answers given were strikingly uniform: Those believing Job Bank gives employers better service cite the broad exposure of openings and resultant faster service. Those saying Job Bank hurts service to employers point to the poorer screening and inability of generalist interviewers to adequately match applicants to openings. Those saying Job Bank doesn't affect employers frequently argued that faster service and poorer screening cancel each other out.

5. The nine counselors interviewed had more positive feelings about Job Bank than did the other respondents. Several noted that having the Job Bank list was very helpful because (a) they no longer had to beg interviewers for openings, (b) they knew for the first time what openings were actually

available, and (c) they had valuable job-market information for counseling use. On balance, counselors even believe that Job Bank helps employers, in marked contrast with the judgment of the other staff members.

6. The four VERs agreed with the majority of the staff that Job Bank helps the disadvantaged, but they perceive that the system reduces service to the nondisadvantaged and to employers. In part, the VERs were responding to focusing on service to the disadvantaged rather than to Job Bank as such. However, one VER said veterans were no longer getting preference, period. All four cited frequent employer complaints concerning the quality of referring, reflecting both efforts to push disadvantaged applicants and the shift toward generalized interviewers.

Summary of Ideas for Improving Job Bank Operations. The following ideas come from three sources: ES staff suggestions for improving Job Bank, state agency management ideas, and appealing things being done in at least one of the Job Bank cities studied.

ES Staff Suggestions for Improving Job Bank

The following suggestions for making the Job Bank system more effective were each mentioned several times.

1. Do more PR and employer relations work to keep orders coming in.
2. Related to 1., do more job development.
3. Go back to specialized order-taking and placement, because there are too many poor-quality referrals this way.
4. As an alternative to 3., increase the amount of information available to placement interviewers. Specifically, take better job orders, add a file of master orders, add a file on each employer, feed ERR reports to placement interviewers.
5. Better control of referral and order status. Too many referrals, referrals on closed orders, delays in finding out about referral outcomes, and old (not recently verified) orders are frequently raised areas.
6. There were several "red tape" complaints, the most common one being the number of phone calls associated with making a referral.
7. It was suggested several times that the Job Bank book should be indexed, segmented, or differently sequenced.

Management Suggestions and Ideas

All of the ideas put forward by staff were also mentioned by one or more management people. However, some additional suggestions emerged, some of which could be better implemented with National Office assistance.

1. The potential of Job Bank for providing management information is simply not being exploited. In part, this is function of programming time, in part design problems, in part low priority it is assigned.
2. Every state is eager to move on to an on-line matching system. They see it as a magic helper and appear in some cases naive about the obstacles.
3. All plan to expand the open-list plus quick referral mode of operation for the job-ready. Experience with this is uniformly good, according to these states.
4. Several states said efforts should be underway now to get a standardized system accepted, so states could relay data back and forth.

Miscellaneous Features

1. Portland uses the Job Bank book as a vehicle for rapid dissemination of messages widely within the organization.
2. Some agencies are concerned with control over job development efforts, i.e., scheduling these calls. A proposed solution is a central control similar to central referral control.

Employer Reactions to the Job Bank: A Report on Interviews in Four Cities: May 12, 1971. The purpose of this study was to gather information concerning employer reactions to Job Banks, to supplement the hard data being collected in the Job Bank Operations Review (JBOR) program (see GAL 1353). Specifically, the study aimed to help determine if employers are reacting adversely to three features of many Job Banks, namely, centralized order-taking, despecialization of referral interviewers, and sharing of job openings with outside Community Agencies.

Study Design

Scope. Interviews were conducted during March and April 1971 in four Job Bank cities. The cities were selected to provide a range of experience on the three Job Bank parameters of special concern as noted above:[c]

1. Philadelphia is characterized by centralized, nonspecialized order-taking; nonspecialized referral interviewing; and heavy participation by Community Agencies. Hence, if the concerns expressed regarding employer reactions to Job Bank are valid, Philadelphia employers should express the greatest dissatisfaction.
2. Oklahoma City also uses centralized, nonspecialized order-taking. However, referral units remain specialized and Community Agency involvement is minimal. Thus any negative employer reactions to the Oklahoma City Job

[c]See Table 1-D for the detailed organizational characteristics of the sample city Job Banks.

Banks can probably be attributed to central order-taking, as this is the major change in the system here.

3. St. Louis has returned to decentralized order-taking by specialized referral interviewers. Further, Community Agency involvement is very limited. Hence, employer attitudes should be positive, relative to the attitudes of employers in other Job Bank cities.

4. Portland has used decentralized order-taking by specialized referral interviewers throughout the time Job Bank has been in use. Community Agency involvement is moderate.

Ten interviewee firms in each city were chosen by local Employment Service management as representative customers, and ten were selected by study staff without regard for their use or lack of use of the ES. Local Chambers of Commerce provided lists of employers from which the latter firms were chosen.

In St. Louis and Portland, the employers interviewed had been asked similar questions about one year earlier, a year after Job Bank had opened in those cities. It is hoped that a comparison of answers to the year-apart interviews will give insight into longer term reactions to Job Bank.

In addition to employers, ES agency management members were interviewed in each city. Typically, the Job Bank manager and the area manager were interviewed.

Methodology & Staffing. A face-to-face, semistructured interview was conducted with each employer. The interviews required fifteen to forty-five minutes each, depending on the responsiveness of the interviewee. Agency management interviews took thirty to sixty minutes.

To assure as much uniformity as possible in the data from various cities, Joseph Ullman worked for at least one day training each interviewer. Specifically, Ullman joined each interviewer in visiting several employers. (In St. Louis and Portland, this training occurred in 1970.)

The interview data were tabulated and analyzed by Joseph Ullman.

Findings

Employer responses from the various cities were summarized and compared in order to learn if employer behavior and/or perceptions were related to differences in the Job Bank attributes of central concern here. The following conclusions resulted from this analysis.

1. Two-thirds (53 of 79) of the employers interviewed had personal or telephone contact with the ES at least once a month, and most of the rest spoke with the ES several times a year. Thus we interviewed mostly employers who used the ES frequently enough to have information on which

to base responses. There were no significant differences among cities in this regard.

2. Employers were generally (72 of 79) satisfied with the promptness of referrals, although only a few perceived any change in the period after Job Bank was implemented. Those perceiving a change were equally divided among those who felt referral was faster and those who believed it was slower after Job Bank. Four or five employers who hire large numbers of workers at one time praised the improvement in referral speed. There were no significant differences among cities in regard to perception of referral promptness.

3. Overall, there appeared to be no significant shift in use of the ES associated with the introduction of Job Bank. Nineteen employers reported less use of the ES because of economic conditions. Eight reported less use due to deterioration of service, but eight others reported more use due to improved service. There were no differences among cities in this regard.

4. Employer awareness of Job Bank appeared to vary among cities, although some of the apparent differences may be due to differences in reporting by various interviewers or to differences in samples. Sixteen of nineteen Philadelphia employers were familiar with Job Bank, compared with eight of twenty Oklahoma City employers. During the previous (1970) study, eight Portland employers showed an awareness that Job Bank existed. Three additional employers were aware of Job Bank this time. Fifteen St. Louis employers showed awareness that Job Bank existed in the 1970 study, and a sixteenth was aware of it at this time.

5. One-third of the sample employers reported a decline in ES contacts for referrals on orders or placing orders. Most of this was associated with a drop in overall hiring activity. Sample employers also reported a slight drop in ES contacts for all other purposes, i.e., job solicitation, Industrial Service, and miscellaneous contacts. Employer perceptions in this area were similar in the various cities.

6. Fewer than one-fourth of the employers reported increased contacts with CAs generally in the past year. Nearly as many reported a decrease, although the drop was almost always attributed to a decline in hiring levels. No employer complained of too many CA contacts, even when he perceived an increase. Perceptions in regard to CA volume of contacts were similar in the various cities.

7. As the above findings indicate, employers in the various sample cities viewed Job Bank similarly in many respects, and use of the Employment Service does not appear to have been affected differentially by the variation in Job Bank form in the four cities.

Despite the apparent consensus in many respects, there was both a quantitative and qualitative variation among employers in different cities in response to the question: "Please suggest some ways the Employment Service could improve its service to your organization."

Philadelphia. Six of the twenty employers interviewed complained specifically about deterioration of applicant screening since Job Bank began. These comments are representative:

> "Must do more prescreening. Before Job Bank we hired one out of three. Now hire one out of five." (Large retailer, heavy user.)[d]

> "Bad matching of people and jobs, especially by Community Agencies. Old specialized system much better. Now just a procurement agency. No relation of people to jobs." (Large manufacturer, heavy user.)

> "Job Bank not fed enough data, so applicants referred don't meet our needs. Also, lost its warm touch. Dealing with IBM cards, not people. Go back to old way." (Utility, light user.)

Two Philadelphia employers said they got *better* service, now that Job Bank was in operation. Both of these firms were concerned primarily with getting a large *quantity* of referrals, however: "We got many more referrals than we used to. Very big improvement." (Large transportation company, light user.)

> "Service has improved. We file jobs requiring a large number of referrals. Screening is excellent." (Large retailer, light user.)

Oklahoma City. Three Oklahoma City employers perceived a deterioration in service since Job Bank:

> "Computer has slowed down referrals. Too much emphasis on disadvantaged now." (Wholesaler, heavy user.)

> "Before, we knew the ES people. Now we've lost personal contact and are not getting as good applicant screening as before." (Retailer, light user.)

> "We used to have very personal contacts with ES, they used to be our friends. We no longer have close relations, so we are getting unqualified applicants. We are tending now to forget about the ES." (Bank, light user.)

In contrast, two employers believed service had improved:

> "We've gotten quicker referrals with Job bank; also, screening seems better." (Retailer, heavy user.)

> "ES now uses a specialized Job Bank. It's a Hell of a good thing. It gets us referrals from all over the city. ES could screen better, but what we want is probably illegal, so screening is as good as possible." (Manufacturer, heavy user.)

Note again, quantity and speed of referral seem of most concern to those liking Job Bank.

---

[d]Defined as obtaining at least 30 percent of hires in at least one broad occupational group through ES.

Portland. No employer noted any change (deterioration or improvement in level of service. However, ten employers said they wished the ES would do a better job of screening. (Eight had made similar comments a year ago.)

There has been no change in the organization of the Portland Job Bank. It is important to point out that the employer complaints of poor screening appear to flow from the fact that the ES is attempting to place disadvantaged applicants in what is currently a very loose labor market. It does not appear that employer dissatisfaction is related to Job Bank. The complaints relate to screening generally, not to a *change* in screening.

St. Louis. Of the six employers who indicated a change of attitude toward ES Service between the 1970 and 1971 studies, five expressed increased satisfaction. In three cases, the perceived improvement was directly related to abandoning central order-taking:

> "I'm glad that tape thing is over, so I can call Mr. _____ again. When Job Bank began, I put in orders and nothing happened." (Manufacturer, heavy user.)

> "I'm very happy they went back to the old system. My friend knows what I want (in terms of applicant characteristics)." (Manufacturer, heavy user.)

> 1970: "Poor matching. They need better job descriptions." 1971: No complaints.

Conclusions

This study found no evidence that employers in any of the cities surveyed are presently making more or less *use* of the Public Employment Service due to their reactions to Job Bank. However, there is evidence that employer *attitudes* toward the ES may be affected differently in the various cities because of variations in Job Bank organization. Thus twice as many Philadelphia employers reacted negatively to Job Bank as was the case in any of the other three cities. Further, the specific comments of some employers in each city supported the fears put forward at the beginning of this section: That centralized order-taking, despecialization of interviewing, and inclusion of Community Agencies would have poor effects on employer relations.

It is clear that the ES management in the various cities are concerned about the effects of Job Bank organization on employers. The following agency-management comments underscore this concern.

On the one hand, is Philadelphia:

> Employers are not enthusiastic. We have a great deal of complaint about centralized order-taking and generalist interviewing because employers like to deal with one person. . . . Some Community Agencies harass employers, and we've had some employer complaints. Overall the ES referral/placement ratio is 5.5/1 versus 6.5/1 for CAs.

In contrast, is Oklahoma City:

> Reaction to the Employment Service is good, but no particular raves on Job Bank as such. No complaints either, however. . . . CAs really haven't done that much, so nothing to say.

Again, in Portland:

> Total concept is well-received, although we get objections to the quality of referrals. . . . Important employers complained about Community Agencies sending unqualified applicants. Two agencies with 9 to 1 referral/placement ratios have been dropped to try to overcome this problem.

Finally, the area manager in St. Louis may have best summed up overall employer reaction to the Job Bank:

> Prior to the shift back to specialized interviewing and decentralized order-taking, employers complained about the lack of personal contact. Now it's hard to get a reading. Employers seem interested in and approving of the *sophistication* of Job Bank, but they are concerned about the *depersonalization*.

The Impact of Job Banks on Employers: An Analysis of the Evidence to Date—May 21, 1971. There has been widespread and intense interest in the impact of Job Banks on employers. This section attempts to pull together the results of the several studies that provide evidence concerning this issue.

Table 1-D

Selected Organizational Characteristics of Sample Job Banks

	St. Louis	Portland	Oklahoma City	Philadelphia
Order-taking				
Percentage taken in central unit	0	0	65%	90%
Specialization within central unit	N.A.	N.A.	None	None
Percentage taken by placement interviewers	100%	100%	35%	10%
Nature of Interviewer Specialization	OI	OI	OI	None
Community Agency Participation				
Number CAs participating	4	23	8	32
Where have access?	ES & own office	own office	own office	own office
Employer ID deleted?	No	No	Yes	No
Percent placement, CA/total?	INA[a]	INA[a]	1%	12%

[a]But less than 1% in spring 1970.

Data Sources

There have been at least four separate employer interview or questionnaire studies aimed at divining the effect of Job Banks on employer use of the Public Employment Service. In chronological order, these studies are:

1. Ullman-Huber I. An interview study covering twenty employers in each of four Job Bank cities (Portland, Seattle, Baltimore, and St. Louis) carried out in spring 1970. The work was done under the supervision of the present authors, while they were working in the MA Division of Manpower Matching Systems. Ten employers in each city were chosen by local ES management as representative customers; and ten more were chosen by study staff as representing area employers generally, not necessarily ES customers.
2. GAO Study. Questionnaire study covering 200 Baltimore employers, conducted by the General Accounting Office in mid-1970.
3. OTS Study. An interview study covering 98 employers in nine cities (Atlanta, Chicago, Dallas, Boston, Philadelphia, Washington, New York, Kansas City, and Seattle). Conducted by MA Office of Technical Support, Division of Occupational Analysis and Employer Services in December 1970.
4. Ullman-Huber II. Similar to Ullman-Huber I, except the cities covered included Philadelphia, Oklahoma City, St. Louis, and Portland. In the latter two cities, the same employers interviewed in Ullman-Huber I were reinterviewed. Study conducted in spring 1971.

In total, the above studies provide reactions to Job Bank from over 400 different employers in thirteen cities. Although this does not provide comprehensive data, the writers believe the scope of the samples was broad enough to be considered probably representative of employer views generally.

In addition to the interview and questionnaire studies cited above, ES operating data from the Job Bank Operations Reviews Program (JBOR) bear on the impact of Job Bank on employers. In the following section, the interview and questionnaire findings are summarized, and then the JBOR data are discussed.

Discussion

Two contrasting impressions emerge from a close reading of the various employer studies: on the one hand, all studies suggest that Job Bank has not affected overall employer *use* of the ES; on the other hand, strong employer criticisms of certain aspects of Job Bank emerge repeatedly in the various studies. The evidence on these two matters, use and criticism, will be presented separately.

Use of the ES under Job Bank. It seems clear from the interview and questionnaire results that Job Bank has had little overall impact on employer use of the Public Employment Service, at least as reported by employers. Relevant summary comments from the four studies follow.

1. Ullman-Huber I. "Overall, employer responses indicated no significant shift in level of use of the Employment Service. Most employers said they used the ES the same amount as before Job Bank, and the slightly larger number of "less" than "more" responses was accounted for by Seattle employers doing less hiring because of the decline in business activity in that area."
2. GAO Study. No direct before-and-after comparison possible, but response to a key question was encouraging: "In the future, do you plan to use, or continue to use the Job Bank as a source for obtaining employees?"

Yes	140
No	45 (But only 13 indicated less use in future than prior to Job Bank)

3. OTS Study. This study was designed to find out what employers want from ES, rather than relative use before and after Job Bank. Nevertheless, several comments indicate continued heavy use: "Generally, about two-thirds of the employers could be identified as regular users of ES placement services. . . . Many employers who do not do so now, would be willing to give their full listings to the ES if we didn't ask for exclusivity or if we contacted them regularly asking for full listings."
4. Ullman-Huber II. "There appeared to be no significant shift in use of the ES associated with the introduction of Job Bank. Nineteen employers reported less use of the ES because of economic conditions. Eight reported less use due to deterioration of service, but eight others reported more use due to improved service."

Employer Criticism of Job Bank. All four of the studies of employer reactions reveal the widespread presence of two complementary criticisms of most forms of Job Bank: depersonalization and poor applicant screening.

1. Ullman-Humber I. "A great deal of criticism of certain aspects of Job Bank emerged from the interviews. . . . The strength of feeling varied widely, but the gist of the complaint is that referral quality drops."
2. GAO Study. Although before-and-after comparison was not elicited by this questionnaire, answers to a question on applicant quality imply considerable criticism of this aspect of Job Bank: "Have you found the individuals sent to you by [Job Bank] to be generally qualified to fill the position to which they were referred?"

Yes	86
No	80
No response	34

3. OTS Study. Major conclusions included "ES screening and orientation of applicants needs improvement"; and some employers "complained of the loss of personal contact that accompanied Job Bank."
4. Ullman-Huber II. "Six of twenty [Philadelphia] employers interviewed complained specifically about deterioration of applicant screening since Job Bank began. . . . It is clear that ES management in the various cities are concerned about the effects of Job Bank organization on employers: we get objections to the quality of referrals; employers like to deal with one person; employers complained about the lack of personal contact."

Impact of Job Bank Organization on the Degree of Employer Criticism

The amount of employer criticism of Job Bank is related to the way in which the particular Job Bank is organized. Specifically, employers are most critical of Job Banks with: (1) centralized order-taking, (2) despecialized referral interviewing, (3) extensive Community Agency participation.

1. Ullman-Huber I. "In three of the four cities studied, placement interviewers are all generalists. Eleven of the 30 ES sample employers and eight of the random sample employers specifically complained about the change from specialized to generalist order-taking and placement interviewers. . . . On the other hand, only two of 10 ES sample and none of 10 random sample employers in the city which retained specialization complained about referral quality, and in these two cases Job Bank was not singled out as the cause of the problem."
2. OTS Study. Summarizing reactions in nine cities, all of which have centralized order-taking and generalist referral interviewers, "The ES needs:

   - Closer contact between ES interviewer and employer
   - Personal touch and industry set-up should be re-established in Job Bank System
   - ES generalists not as capable as specialists for working with professional applicants
   - ES interviewers should be more knowledgeable of employer requirements
   - Better screening of applicants before referral."

3. Ullman-Huber II. The specific comments of some employers in each of the four cities support the fear that centralized order-taking, despecialized interviewing, and inclusion of Community Agencies would have poor effects on employer relations. Comments of agency managements suggest similar concerns:

   "We have a great deal of complaint about centralized order-taking and generalist interviewing. . . . Overall ES referral/placement ratio is 5.5/1 versus 6.5/1 for Community Agencies."

"Important employers complained about Community Agencies sending un-qualified applicants. Two agencies with 9 to 1 referral placement ratios have been dropped."

"Prior to our shift back to specialized interviewing and order-taking, em-ployers complained about the lack of personal contact."

Conclusion

It is clear that employer criticism of the Job Bank is less in cities retaining specialized referral interviewing and order-taking. It also appears that criticism is less in cities with less Community Agency involvement.

On the basis of this evidence, unless there are offsetting considerations, the Manpower Administration would be well-advised to promote a Job Bank model retaining specialization and personalized relationships and down playing Community Agency involvement.

Obtaining Design Data:
The Operations Flow Study

As described in Chapter 4, during the spring of 1970 there was a good deal of discussion taking place within DMMS concerning the effect of several organizational design variables. The present researchers, having conducted the first of the interview studies, were especially aware of the testimonial evidence suggesting that some levels of these variables were perceived by some Job Bank staff and clients to be much more functional than others. Because of our background in inference statistics, we were also especially cognizant of the fact that these beliefs could be tested if data on the design configurations of the cities providing JBOR performance data could be obtained.

Accordingly, we suggested to the chief of DMMS that such data be collected from the Job Banks. After some discussion and the request for a rough draft of the questionnaire, he agreed to collect the data. Because the researchers left the National Office in June and because the chief and his staff had items of local configuration information that they were interested in learning more about, the design and implementation of the questionnaire were carried out by DMMS staff. The questionnaires were mailed in September of 1970, and those that were completed were returned later that fall. An example questionnaire is contained in Appendix 4.

Completion of this questionnaire was not made mandatory, probably because (1) of the high organizational cost of getting it made mandatory, and (2) DMMS had used up a great many of its political credits in getting JBOR made mandatory. It was routed through the regional offices by DMMS with a request for their cooperation in obtaining the data. Through this mechanism, organizational design data were obtained on eighteen of the twenty-two Job Banks that had returned JBOR data. In order to relate the findings concerning goal achievement quite directly to the findings concerning optimal design, it was decided to use these eighteen cities as the data base for both sets of analyses.

Analyzing the Data and Drawing
Conclusions

Identifying Relationships. Although we used eighteen Job Bank cities in our statistical analysis of optimal design configuration, for the following reasons fewer cities may have been used in any particular computer run: (1) for February, there were just seventeen cities that reported usable data, and in March there were just fifteen; (2) particular combinations of performance measures and design variables required that certain cities be deleted due to unreported data; and (3) while in many tests for relationships we included the four cities in which the "Conceptual Model" (COMO) arrangement was operating simultaneously with the Job Bank, we always duplicated these tests and in addition ran other tests where these cities were not included. As a consequence of these factors, the number of cities included varied from run to run.

Three control variables were also examined for their effect on pre-to-post Job Bank changes in performance. These were population, change in unemployment, and startup date of the Job Bank. Altogether, then, there were twenty-one independent variables to run against any particular dependent variable. We ran almost all combinations of independent and dependent variables in order to find any unhypothesized relationships between the design variables and relative goal achievement. The primary statistical technique used was simple linear regression. We used it rather than multiple regression for the following reasons: (1) we were short on degrees of freedom and the addition of other independent variables would make this problem even more acute, especially since additional independent variables would sometimes cause additional cities to be eliminated; (2) in view of the fact that for most performance measures we had potentially more independent variables than we had observations, we would have had to run simple linear regressions anyway in order to perform the initial screening out of independent variables; and (3) the results obtained from simple regression runs were viewed as being more meaningful to the program administrators.

In order to aid in determining if some of the effects thought to be caused by the design variables were really caused by their being highly correlated with other design variables or with the control variables, we also ran correlations among all independent variables. Very few of these correlations were significant at the 0.05 level. When they were, the possible effects on the relationship between the corresponding independent variables and the performance measures were examined in more detail, using multiple regression and/or studying the direction and relative magnitude of the effects.

Drawing Conclusions.[17] It is important to note that our interview studies and the survey studies described in the previous section had generated some very strong hypotheses. While we did run nearly all combinations of independent and dependent variables to make sure that we had not overlooked any important relationships, we were primarily interested in determining if hard data would support the hypotheses developed from interviews with Job Bank staff and clients. The interview data had had relatively little impact on the direction and structure of the program, except to cause the program administrators to grant more flexibility to the individual cities in the design configuration. We were interested in knowing if the combination of hard data and interview data, assuming that they were supportive of each other, would have more of an impact.

The results of our analyses are shown in Appendix 2. A significance level of 0.20 was used to screen the results for reporting purposes. In order to draw conclusions regarding the effect of an individual design feature on a Job Bank goal, we studied the number and level of significant relationships between the design feature and the several performance measures related to the Job Bank goal and examined the logic that would cause a correlational relationship to be interpreted as a causal relationship. Our reasoning for reaching each of our conclusions concerning optimal design is detailed in Chapter 3. (See the section "Findings Underlying the Recommendations.")

Strictly speaking, our findings concerning optimal design apply only to these eighteen Job Banks. The differences between these and the other Job Banks are discussed in the earlier subsection "Drawing Conclusions," p. 85. It does not appear that these differences should affect our conclusions concerning which design variables are important—i.e., it is difficult to see why there should be much relationship between cooperativeness with the National Office and the effect of design features on local Job Bank operation. In addition, our conclusions were based on the interview and survey studies described earlier, and these included cities not in our eighteen.

Assessing the Impact of Feedback

Assessing the impact of feedback of research results on program administration and administrators was a two-step task. These two tasks were undertaken concurrently.

Obtaining Information about Decisions

One step was to develop and maintain a record of all known decisions pertaining to the Job Bank Program together with the reasons for the decisions insofar as we could determine these. To the extent possible, other pertinent information, namely the date of the decision, the names of the person or persons making the decision, the manner in which the decision was codified, and the empirical evidence available to the decision-makers, was also ascertained and recorded. Because the tracking of program decisions was expected to be a formidable job, considerable care was taken to assure that we become aware of decisions and the surrounding circumstances. All written records in DMMS were made available to the researchers and these records were carefully examined. The available records included not only the various periodic reports of the division to higher levels of organization, but also DMMS files relating to the origin of the Division and the complete chronological correspondence file. The chronological file was examined from its beginning at the origin of DMMS through June 1972.

The written records were supplemented by discussions with several levels of Manpower Administration officials. On the one hand, these discussions were used to obtain the details surrounding decisions we discovered in our search of written records. On the other hand, the periodic discussions with various officials revealed whether or not there had been additional decisions made of which we were unaware.

The discussions of decisions occurred periodically through most of our tenure in DMMS, as well as during the period after we left the Manpower Administration. Although we felt confident that sufficient care had been taken to assure that we had the required information concerning decisions made prior to our leaving the MA, we had some concern that we might not learn of all subsequent decisions. As matters developed, this did not become a problem as the basic direction of the Job Bank Program did not change between our departure and June 1972, the end of the period with which this research is conceived. Hence, we needed only to learn the bases of the decisions concerning Job Bank design, and these were relatively easy to ascertain because we had frequent direct contact with those responsible for such decisions.

There was one area of decision-making for which we do not have data, although this also turned out not to present a problem. We do not know what decisions were made above the level of USTES concerning the allocation of funds between Job Banks and other programs. However, because we are virtually certain that most of our findings concerning Job Bank goal achievement did not reach levels above USTES, we presume the feedback had no affect above USTES and therefore decision-making above USTES need not concern us.

Providing Feedback

The second step in assessing the impact of the feedback of research results was to periodically provide USTES officials with analyses of data bearing on Job Bank performance and optimum design. As noted elsewhere, this feedback was accomplished through a series of five meetings held between March 1971 and June 1972. At these meetings we presented our findings and recommendations and noted the reactions of the various USTES officials to them. Although there was some variation in our stance, we generally took a position at these meetings of advocate for the recommendations. In addition to presenting findings and advocating adoption of our recommendations, we inquired (as did ORD officials) in these meetings as to what action was being taken as a result of our research results. Given that the USTES official was aware that one purpose of the research was to assess the impact of findings on program administration, it is certainly possible that the research affected the administrators in a Hawthorne effect sense. Thus our findings and conclusions may relate more to the question "*Can* feedback affect program administration?" than to the question "*Does* feedback affect program administration?"

Our decision to intervene in the research as advocates was a conscious one. We based the decision on the realization that feedback does not usually have an effect,[18] and our associated belief that it was reasonable to test the question in a "Can" sense.

It may be that the above argument overstates the impact of the research qua research on the administrators. We certainly do not believe we were manipulating these administrators (indeed, it was occasionally suggested to us by ORD officials that the reverse was true, but we believe a small impact may have resulted strictly from the nature of the research.

Analyzing the Feedback Effect and
Drawing Conclusions

Our approach to analyzing the effect of feedback and drawing conclusions was based on two straight forward ideas. First, if feedback did not reach relevant decision-makers, we concluded that it had "no effect." Second, if a decision was made by someone who had feedback available, and if the decision-maker told us or if there was written evidence to the effect that the feedback affected the decision, we concluded that the feedback had had an effect. Although these decision rules were unsophisticated, we could not think of any other approaches that were more appropriate.

We also probed the circumstances surrounding each decision ourselves in an effort to determine why equally valid data feedback did not always have equal impact. In this way, we attempted to deduce circumstances under which research feedback is most likely to have an effect. The results of this probing are reported in the first section of Chapter 5.

Appendix 2: Determining Optimal Job Bank Design Configuration

Appendix A: Definitions and Job Bank City Characteristics

Good, Bad, and Total Jobs

In order to determine if Job Banks differentially effect jobs in different skill categories, separate analyses were made of "Good," "Bad," and "Total" jobs. "Total" jobs were in fact all placements, referrals, etc.

"Good" jobs included all placements and referrals in the following DOT occupational categories (first two digits for 20, 31, and 38; first and fourth digits in other categories).

20 Stenography, typing, filing.
62 Machine trades—analyzing relation to data.
67 Machine trades—no significant relation to data; at least operating or controlling relation to things.
77 Bench work—no significant relation to data; at least operating or controlling relation to things.
87 Structural work—no significant relation to data; at least operating or controlling relation to things.

"Poor" jobs included all placements and referrals in these DOT codes:

31 Food and beverage service and preparation.
38 Building and related service occupations.
68 Machine Trades—no significant relation to data; less than operating or controlling relation to things.
78 Bench work—no significant relation to data; less than operating or controlling relation to things.
88 Structural work—no significant relation to data; less than operating or controlling relation to things.
98 Miscellaneous work—no significant relation to data; less than operating or controlling relation to things.

COMO In and COMO Out

In initial analyses of data, COMO cities tended to yield different results than other cities.[1] In statistical parlance, they tended to be "outliers." Because of

Table 2-A
Job Bank City Characteristics

City	Months Included Feb	Mar	Order-Taking Spec	NS	Referral Spec	NS	Output Hard	Other	CAs 0-2	3+	Books/Int Cl	1+	Multi-Service Lo	Hi	Poverty Area Lo	Hi	Bifur Err's Lo	Hi	Con-tinuous Err's	First-Day Placement +	–	Number of ES Offices	Openings Filled Same Day (1971)
Albuquerque		X		X	X		X			X		X	X	X	X	X	X		.098		X	3	.328
Birmingham	X	X	X	X	INA		X		X	X		X	X		X			X	.119		X	3	.177
Buffalo	X	X		X	X			X	X			X		X		X	X		.063		X	7	.295
Cincinnati	X	X		X	X			X	X	X	X	X	X	X	X	X	X		.055		X	5	.186
Cleveland	X	X	X		X			X	X	X	X	X	X	X	X	X	X		.060	X		4	.293
Columbia	X	X		X	X		X			X		X	X		X		X		.051		X	2	.296
Columbus	X	X		X	X					X		X	X		X		X		.027	X		2	.162
Des Moines	X	X	INA		X			X	X			X	X	X	X	X		X	.129	X		1	.136
Hartford	X	X	X	X	X		X		X		X			X		X	X		.024	X		16	.305
Little Rock	X	X	X		X		X		X		X			X		X	X		.038	X		6	.521
Minneapolis	X		X		X			X	X			X	INA		INA		INA		INA	X		3	.599
Oklahoma City	X	X	X		X			X	X			X	X		X		X		.027		X	5	.496
Omaha	X	X	X		X			X	X			X	INA		INA		INA		INA	X		11	.210
Tulsa	X	X		X	X			X	X			X		X		X	X		.025		X	2	.485
Memphis[a]	X	X	X	X	X		X		X			X	X		X			X	.155		X	INA	.209
Phoenix[a]	X	X	X			X			X			X		X		X		X	.130		X	18	.126
Syracuse[a]	X	X	X	X	INA		X		X			X		X		X		X	.168		X	1	.175
Wichita[a]	X	X		X		X		X	X			X		X		X		X	.121	INA		5	INA

[a]COMO City

	Organizational Variables						Control Variables			
	Months Included		Change in Openings Filled Same Day		Referrals Verified by Interviewers	Referrals Verified by Phone by Central Unit	Increase in Unemployment		1970 SMSA Population (000)	Months from Jan., 1970 to Job Bank Start
City	Feb	Mar	+	–			0-1.3%	Over 1.3%		
Albuquerque		X		X	.05	.10	X		316	6
Birmingham	X	X		X	.69	.00	X		739	5
Buffalo	X	X		X	INA	INA		X	1349	6
Cincinnati	X	X		X	.00	.45		X	1385	6
Cleveland	X	X	X		.05	.65		X	2064	6
Columbia	X	X		X	.40	.00			323	6
Columbus	X	X	X		.05	.27	X		916	3
Des Moines	X	X		X	.05	.95	X		284	6
Hartford	X		X		INA	INA		X	664	3
Little Rock	X	X	X		.30	INA	X		323	5
Minneapolis	X		X		.08	.01		X	1814	3
Oklahoma City	X	X		X	1.00	.00	X		641	6
Omaha	X	X	X		.01	.00	X		541	6
Tulsa	X	X		X	1.00	.00		X	476	6
Memphis[a]	X	X		X	.00	INA	X		770	4
Phoenix[a]	X	X		X	.05	.95		X	968	4
Syracuse[a]	X	X		X	INA	INA		X	636	5
Wichita[a]	X	X	INA		.21	.78		X	389	5

[a]COMO City

this, many subsequent analyses were made excluding COMO cities. Our conclusions and recommendations are based on this dual analysis, i.e., COMO in our data and COMO not in.

Appendix B: Key Data Relating to Analysis of Achievement of Program Goals

B-1. Key Data Relating to More Efficient Matching
(All Values Are Changes from 1970 to 1971)

a) Change in Referral/Regular Placement Ratio's (Table I)

		Job Banks	Comparison Cities	S.l.[a]
February	COMO in	1.35	—	—
	COMO out	0.90	1.70	.38
March	COMO in	1.26	—	—
	COMO out	0.34	0.59	.73

JB vs. CC differences are not statistically significant at the 5% level.

b) Proportionate Change in Number of Referrals (Table I)

		Job Banks	Comparison Cities	S.l.
February	COMO in	−0.2%	—	—
	COMO out	−2.9	−14.5	.53
March	COMO in	—	—	—
	COMO out	22.1	−17.4	.09

Referrals declined marginally less in Job Banks than in comparison cities in March.

c) Proportionate Change in Number of Placements and Regular Placements

February		Table	Job Banks	Comparison Cities	U.S.	S.l.
Regular	COMO in, I		−26.5%	—	—	—
Regular	COMO in, VII		−34.8	—	—	—
Regular	COMO out, I		−21.4	−24.7	—	.74
Total	COMO out, VII		−38.1	−19.3	−21.1	.02

[a]S.L.—Significance level, the probability that the JB vs CC difference could have occurred by chance alone, given the variability among the individual data values (two-tailed test).

March

Regular	COMO in, I	− 3.5	—	—	—
Regular	COMO in, VII	−12.2	—	—	—
Regular	COMO out, I	0.5	− 4.5	—	.50
Total	COMO out, VII	−15.4	− 1.4	−10.0	.11

JB vs. CC Regular Placements differences are not statistically significant at the 5% level.

JB vs. CC and JB vs. US Placements differences are statistically significant at the 5% level for February and nearly so for March.

d) Change in Total Placements/New Applications Ratio (Table VII)

		Job Banks	Comparison Cities	U.S.	S.1.
February	COMO in	−11.8%	—	—	—
	COMO out	−18.0	11.4%	(38.6 to 31.5) −7.1	.23
March	COMO in	− 2.3	—	—	—
	COMO out	−10.2	−10.2	(39.6 to 35.5) −4.1	.99

JB vs. CC differences are not statistically significant at the 5% level.

JB vs. US differences are statistically significant at the 5% level.

e) Change in Total Placement/Openings Received Ratio (Table VII)

		Job Banks	Comparison Cities	U.S.	S.1.
February	COMO in	−11.4%	—	—	—
	COMO out	−10.5	−2.4%	(67.2 to 63.9) −3.3	.14
March	COMO in	−13.1	—	—	—
	COMO out	−14.1	−7.8	(63.8 to 59.6) −4.2	.26

JB vs. CC differences are not statistically significant at the 5% level.

JB vs. US differences are statistically significant at the 5% level.

f) Effect of Job Bank on Average Wages

	Job Bank Wages			BLS Wages in Manufacturing		
	ave. 1970	ave. 1971	% change	ave. 1970	ave. 1971	% change
February	$2.05	$2.09	+1.5%	$3.29	$3.51	+6.7%
March	1.95	2.08	+6.0%	3.31	3.52	+6.3%

Although year-to-year change in Job Bank wages is significant in March, the change is not greater than the average change in manufacturing wages.

g) Effect of Job Bank on Proportion of Regular Placements in Jobs Paying More than $2.50 per Hour (Table IV)

	Job Banks	Comparison Cities
February COMO in	0.4%	—
March COMO in	7.4%	—

Year-to-year change is different from zero at the 5% level in March, but not in February.

B-2. Key Data Relating to More Efficient Matching, Corrected for the Effect of Population by Deleting Most Populous Job Banks and Least Populous Comparison Cities (COMO Out, Only)

a) Change in Referral/Regular Placement Ratios (Table I)

	Job Banks	Comparison Cities	S.L.
March	.297	−.507	.12

b) Proportionate Change in Number of Placements

	Job Banks	Comparison Cities	S.L.
February, Table VII	−37.2%	−12.8%	.00
March, Table VII	−12.6%	+ 8.6	.01

c) Change in Total Placements/Openings Received Ratio (Table VII)

	Job Banks	Comparison Cities	S.L.
March	−15.3%	− 4.7%	.09

d) Change in Number of Openings Received (Table VII)

	Job Banks	Comparison Cities	S.L.
February	−26.8%	−10.4%	.06

e) Change in Number of New Application (Table VII)

	Job Banks	Comparison Cities	S.L.
March	26.3%	4.7%	.09

B-3. Key Data Relating to Service to the Disadvantaged
(All Values Are Changes from 1970 to 1971)

a) Proportionate Change in Number of Regular Placements (Table I)

		Job Banks	Comparison Cities	U.S.	S.L.
February	COMO in DIS	−27.2%	—	—	—
	NDIS	−24.2	—	—	—
	COMO out DIS	−16.6	−24.4%	−24.9%	.79
	NDIS	−20.9	−23.1	−20.1	.86
March	COMO in DIS	53.2	—	—	—
	NDIS	− 5.1	—	—	—
	COMO out DIS	22.8[a]	−14.6	− 5.0	.42
	NDIS	− 3.4	− 3.9	−11.9	.97

[a]Primarily due to increase of 223% in Des Moines.

JB vs. CC differences are not statistically significant at the 5% level.

b) Change in Ratio of Disadvantaged Persons Placed to Total Persons Placed, Regular Placements (Table I)

		Job Banks
February	COMO in	−1.8%
	COMO out	−1.1
March	COMO in	3.0
	COMO out	2.2

Year to year differences not significantly different from 0 at 5% level.

c) Change in Referral/Regular Placement Ratios (Table I)

			Job Banks
February	COMO in	DIS	1.37
		NDIS	1.44
	COMO out	DIS	.89
		NDIS	1.01
March	COMO in	DIS	1.32
		NDIS	1.37
	COMO out	DIS	1.10
		NDIS	.81

d) Change in Ratio of Total Placements to New Applications (Table VII)

			Job Banks	Comparison Cities	U.S.	S.L.
February	COMO in	DIS	−29.0%	—	—	—
		NDIS	− 7.7	—	—	—
	COMO out	DIS	− 6.2	−18.7%	(54.3% to 40.9%) −13.4%	.45
		NDIS	−20.4	−10.3	(35.8% to 29.8%) − 6.0%	.11
March	COMO in	DIS	− 7.0	—	—	—
		NDIS	− 1.2	—	—	—
	COMO out	DIS	4.5	3.7	(53.0% to 47.9%) − 5.1%	.92
		NDIS	−11.1	− 8.1	(37.1% to 32.9%) − 4.2%	.54

JB vs. CC differences are not statistically significant at the 5% level.

JB vs. US differences are statistically significant at the 5% level.

e) Change in Proportion of Regular Placements in Jobs Paying More Than $2.50 per Hour (Table IV)

			Job Banks	
February	COMO in	DIS	1.2%	(13.5% vs. 14.7%)
		NDIS	0.6	(23.9 vs. 24.5)
March	COMO in	DIS	9.4	(8.1 vs. 17.5)
		NDIS	7.0	(17.4 vs. 24.4)

Differences between Disadvantaged and Nondisadvantaged are not statistically significantly different from 0 at the 5% level.

f) Change in Proportion of Regular Placements in Good DOT Jobs (Table I)

			Job Banks	
February	COMO in	DIS	1.1%	(8.8% vs. 9.9%)
		NDIS	1.2	(12.5 vs. 13.7)
	COMO out	DIS	0.4	
		NDIS	1.0	
March	COMO in	DIS	−0.6	(8.7 vs. 8.1)
		NDIS	1.7	(12.1 vs. 13.8)
	COMO out	DIS	−2.6	
		NDIS	1.0	

Change in proportion in over $2.50 jobs and in good jobs is not correlated with unemployment rate.

Year to year differences are not statistically significantly different from 0 at the 5% level.

B-4. Key Data Relating to Overall Activity Measures
(All Values Are Changes from 1970 to 1971)

See page B-1, item c) for data pertaining to placements and regular placements.

a) Proportionate Change in Number of Openings Received

	Job Banks	Comparison Cities	U.S.	S.L.
February	−25.7%	−17.3%		.31
			−17.1%	.25
March	+ 5.8%	+ 7.8%		.83
			− 1.9%	.15

JB vs. CC and JB vs. US Openings Received differences are not statistically significant at the 5% level.

b) Proportionate Change in Number of New Applications

	Job Banks	Comparison Cities	U.S.	S.L.
February	+ 0.8%	+ 7.0%		.64
			−3.4%	.64
March	+17.9%	+25.8%		.67
			+0.6%	.16

JB vs. CC and JB vs. US New Applications differences are not statistically significant at the 5% level.

Appendix C: Significant Differences in
Operating Data Associated with Various
Organizational and Control Variables

Each organizational attribute and control variable was bifurcated (0,1) and correlated with each of thirty performance variables. Some variables were also run in continuous form. As in any such analysis, only a few correlations were statistically significant. All correlations significant at the 0.20 level are shown. (The 0.20 level means that the results could have occurred by chance alone only 20 percent of the time.)

For many organizational attribute-performance variable pairs, a number of correlations were run: in many cases, separate correlations were considered for disadvantaged, nondisadvantaged, and total applicants. Within each applicant group "Good" jobs, "Bad" jobs, and "all" jobs were considered. The following code is used here to refer to the various groups:

DIS B	=	Disadvantaged applicants–Bad jobs
DIS G	=	Disadvantaged applicants–Good jobs
DIS T	=	Disadvantaged applicants–All jobs
NDIS B	=	Nondisadvantaged applicants–Bad jobs
NDIS G	=	Nondisadvantaged applicants–Good jobs
NDIS T	=	Nondisadvantaged applicants–All jobs
TOT B	=	All applicants–Bad jobs
TOT G	=	All applicants–Good jobs
TOT T	=	All applicants–All jobs

Each of these correlations was run for February and March separately, and in most cases both with COMO cities in and with COMO cities out. Hence, there were thirty-six (nine times two months times two runs) correlations run for many organizational attribute-performance variable pairs.

"COMO in" is coded CI and "COMO out" CO in the following listings.

Organizational Variables

ORG. 1) Specialized vs. Nonspecialized Order-taking

a) Change in referral/placement ratios tends to be higher in nonspecialized cities.

			Significance Level	Base Levels for This Variable
Feb - CI -	DIS	G	.20	(0.90 vs. 3.28)
(4/9)[a]	TOT	G	.11	(0.03 vs. 2.86)
	TOT	B	.09	(0.29 vs. 1.82)
	TOT	T	.15	(0.69 vs. 1.92)

[a](4/9) means that four correlations were statistically significant at the 0.20 level or better out of nine tests. That is, four were significant and five were not significant at the 0.20 level.

Feb - CO -	NDIS G	.17	(0.05 vs. 2.43)
(3/9)	NDIS B	.11	(0.23 vs. 1.87)
	TOT B	.19	(0.02 vs. 1.37)
Mar - CI -	DIS B	.13	(0.51 vs. 2.52)
(3/9)	DIS T	.10	(0.25 vs. 2.07)
	TOT B	.13	(0.69 vs. 2.11)
Mar - CO -	DIS B	.03	(−0.32 vs. 1.92)
(4/9)	DIS T	.06	(−0.43 vs. 1.87)
	NDIS B	.18	(0.80 vs. 2.06)
	TOT B	.11	(0.16 vs. 1.76)

ORG. 2) Specialized vs. Nonspecialized Referral

a) Change in placements down most in nonspecialized.
   (All non-COMO Job Banks were specialized)

Feb - CI	DIS T	.15	(−0.19 vs. −0.73)
(6/9)	NDIS G	.16	(0.04 vs. −0.55)
	NDIS T	.05	(−0.19 vs. −0.56)
	TOT G	.11	(−0.05 vs. −0.59)
	TOT B	.19	(−0.19 vs. −0.50)
	TOT T	.03	(−0.20 vs. −0.59)
Mar - CI -	NDIS G	.11	(0.05 vs. 0.86) ⎫ reverse
(2/9)	TOT G	.10	(0.07 vs. 1.08) ⎭

b) Referral/placement ratios rose most in nonspecialized.
   (All non-COMO Job Banks were specialized)

		Significance Level	Base Levels for This Variable
Feb - CI -	DIS B	.10	(1.05 vs. 3.13)
(8/9)	DIS T	.00	(0.91 vs. 3.90)
	NDIS G	.00	(0.41 vs. 6.42)
	NDIS B	.14	(0.79 vs. 2.89)
	NDIS T	.06	(1.06 vs. 3.51)
	TOT G	.00	(0.52 vs. 7.26)
	TOT B	.08	(0.78 vs. 2.95)
	TOT T	.02	(0.95 vs. 3.56)
Mar - CI -	NDIS G	.03	(1.46 vs. 7.88)
(3/9)	DIS T	.11	(0.91 vs. 2.81)
	TOT T	.18	(0.87 vs. 2.49)

ORG. 3) Ratio of FTE Employer Relations Representatives to FTE Placement Personnel (Bifurcated Variable)

a) Change in proportion of applicants placed is higher where FTE Employer Relations Representatives proportion is higher.

Feb -	DIS	T	.13	(−0.57 vs. 0.18)
(3/3)	NDIS	T	.04	(−0.16 vs. 0.13)
	TOT	T	.00	(−0.22 vs. 0.07)
March -	NDIS	T	.14	(−0.13 vs. 0.23)
(2/3)	TOT	T	.13	(−0.09 vs. 0.12)

b) Increase in proportion of placements in $2.50 per hour or more jobs is greater where FTE Employer Relations Representative proportion is higher.

March -	DIS	T	.06	(0.04 vs. 0.15)
(3/3)	NDIS	T	.03	(0.04 vs. 0.10)
	TOT	T	.02	(0.04 vs. 0.11)

ORG. 4) Ratio of Number of Employer Relations Personnel to FTE Placement Personnel (Continuous Variable)

(Based only on COMO in, as too little variance elsewhere)

a) Increase in proportion placed greater, or decrease lower, where ERR proportion higher.

			Significance Level	Base Level for This Variable
Feb -	DIS	T	.13	
(3/3)	NDIS	T	.02	
	TOT	T	.00	
March -	NDIS	T	.09	
(2/3)	TOT	T	.17	

ORG. 5) Number of Associated Community Agencies

a) Referrals declined more in cities with three or more CAs than in other cities.

Feb - CI -	DIS	B	.02	(0.55 vs. −0.18)
(8/9)	DIS	T	.09	(0.38 vs. −0.17)
	NDIS	G	.00	(0.60 vs. −0.17)

			Significance Level	Base Level for This Variable
	NDIS	B	.02	(0.28 vs. −0.11)
	NDIS	T	.04	(0.31 vs. −0.05)
	TOT	G	.00	(0.58 vs. −0.16)
	TOT	B	.01	(0.29 vs. −0.14)
	TOT	T	.03	(0.31 vs. −0.09)
Feb - CO -	DIS	B	.07	(0.53 vs. −0.22)
(8/9)	DIS	T	.15	(0.42 vs. −0.18)
	NDIS	G	.00	(0.64 vs. −0.26)
	NDIS	B	.00	(0.33 vs. −0.22)
	NDIS	T	.01	(0.34 vs. −0.15)
	TOT	G	.00	(0.54 vs. −0.25)
	TOT	B	.00	(0.33 vs. −0.24)
	TOT	T	.02	(0.34 vs. −0.18)
Mar - CO -	DIS	T	.05	(0.69 vs. 0.09)
(1/9)				

b) Placements declined more, especially in good jobs, where three or more CAs.

			Significance Level	Base Level for This Variable
Feb - CO -	DIS	G	.01	(0.24 vs. −0.43)
(5/9)	NDIS	G	.07	(0.37 vs. −0.23)
	TOT	G	.04	(0.32 vs. −0.26)
	TOT	B	.16	(0.04 vs. −0.28)
	TOT	T	.16	(−0.07 vs. −0.28)
Mar - CO -	DIS	G	.08	(0.75 vs. −0.40)
(1/9)				

c) Disadvantaged proportion of total placements less where there were three or more CAs.

Mar - CI -	TOT	B	.05	(0.13 vs. −0.01)
(2/3)	TOT	T	.01	(0.14 vs. −0.01)
Mar - CO -	TOT	B	.13	(0.08 vs. −0.03)
(2/3)	TOT	T	.01	(0.10 vs. −0.03)

d) Proportion of placement in $2.50 per hour or more jobs rose less or declines more in cities with three or more CAs.

Feb - CI -	DIS	T	.03	(0.13 vs. 0.04)
(3/3)	NDIS	T	.05	(0.09 vs. −0.03)
	TOT	T	.02	(0.10 vs. −0.03)

Mar - CI -	DIS	T	.01	(0.19 vs. 0.04)
(2/3)	TOT	T	.11	(0.11 vs. 0.06)

e) Proportion of placements in high and medium-skill jobs declined more where three or more CAs.

Feb - CI -	NDIS	T	.10	(0.04 vs. −0.00)
(2/3)	TOT	T	.17	(0.04 vs. 0.00)
Feb - CO -	NDIS	T	.03	(0.06 vs. −0.01)
(2/3)	TOT	T	.05	(0.05 vs. −0.01)

ORG. 6) Books or Video Terminals per Interviewer

a) Placements declined more in cities with fewer books per interviewer.

			Significance Level	Base Level for This Variable
Feb - CI -	DIS	G	.16	(0.28 vs. −0.33)
(7/9)	NDIS	G	.03	(0.22 vs. −0.32)
	NDIS	B	.13	(0.05 vs. −0.33)
	NDIS	T	.03	(−0.05 vs. −0.36)
	TOT	G	.02	(0.20 vs. −0.34)
	TOT	B	.09	(−0.06 vs. −0.35)
	TOT	T	.02	(−0.08 vs. −0.38)
Feb - CO -	NDIS	G	.10	(0.26 vs. −0.25)
(6/9)	NDIS	B	.17	(0.14 vs. −0.28)
	NDIS	T	.11	(−0.04 vs. −0.29)
	TOT	G	.13	(0.17 vs. −0.26)
	TOT	B	.15	(0.00 vs. −0.30)
	TOT	T	.07	(−0.08 vs. −0.31)
Mar - CO -	DIS	G	.11	(0.57 vs. −0.45)
(1/9)				

b) Referral/placement ratios increased more in cities with fewer books per interviewer, especially for good jobs.

Feb - CI -	NDIS	G	.05	(−0.74 vs. 2.63)
(4/9)	NDIS	B	.11	(0.10 vs. 1.55)
	NDIS	T	.12	(0.50 vs. 2.02)
	TOT	G	.08	(−0.42 vs. 2.89)
Feb - CO -	DIS	B	.04	(2.24 vs. 0.18) ⎫ reverse
(4/9)	DIS	T	.02	(1.72 vs. 0.32) ⎭
	NDIS	G	.14	(−0.81 vs. 1.37)

	NDIS	B	.17	(−0.31 vs. 1.37)
	NDIS	T	.20	(0.23 vs. 1.53)
	TOT	G	.20	(−0.36 vs. 1.30)
Mar - CI -	DIS	G	.01	(−0.25 vs. 4.66)
(3/9)	NDIS	G	.12	(0.37 vs. 1.67)
	TOT	G	.05	(0.17 vs. 1.76)
Mar - CO -	DIS	G	.01	(0.04 vs. 3.37)
(3/9)	NDIS	G	.05	(−0.18 vs. 1.81)
	TOT	G	.03	(−0.21 vs. 1.93)

ORG. 7) Ratio of Full-Time Equivalent FTE Staff in Multiservice Centers to FTE Total Placement Staff

a) Referral/placement ratio for good jobs higher where multiservice proportion is higher.

			Significance Level		Base Level for This Variable
Feb - CO -	DIS	G	.08		(4.46 vs. 0.23)
(3/3)	DIS	B	.05	lower	(2.57 vs. 0.19)
	DIS	T	.07		(1.72 vs. 0.40)
Mar - CI -	DIS	G	.12		(0.28 vs. 3.77)
(3/3)	NDIS	G	.07	higher	(0.18 vs. 1.77)
	TOT	G	.02		(−0.03 vs. 1.83)
Mar - CO -	NDIS	G	.02		(−0.91 vs. 1.67)
(2/3)	TOT	G	.04	higher	(−0.78 vs. 1.67)

b) Openings received fell more in cities with high FTE proportion in multiservice centers.

Feb - CI -	.06	(−0.04 vs. −0.31)
(1/1)		
Mar - CI -		
(1/1)	.19	(0.22 vs. 0.06)

ORG. 8) Ratio of FTE Staff in Poverty Areas to FTE Placement Personnel

a) Placements declined more in cities with more FTE in poverty areas.

Feb. - CO -	DIS	G	.17	declined	(−0.31 vs. 0.07)
(2/9)	DIS	B	.15	less	(−0.44 vs. −0.03)

Mar - CI -	NDIS B	.07	(0.03 vs. −0.27)
(5/9)	NDIS T	.03	(0.08 vs. −0.31)
	TOT G	.16	(0.48 vs. −0.16)
	TOT B	.04	(0.15 vs. −0.28)
	TOT T	.03	(0.21 vs. −0.29)

{.03, .16, .04} declined more

b) Time to fill openings declined more in cities with high FTE in poverty areas, due in part to coincidence of unemployment rate positive correlation with FTE in poverty areas.

		Significance Level	Base Level for This Variable
Feb - Openings	G	.04	(4.94 vs. −4.26)
(3/3)	B	.07	(4.34 vs. −4.57)
	T	.02	(2.06 vs. −7.17)
Mar - Openings	G	.18	(2.16 vs. −1.26)
(3/3)	B	.01	(3.53 vs. −4.90)
	T	.00	(1.52 vs. −4.52)

ORG. 9) Hard Copy vs. Video Display Communications Devices

a) Placements down significantly less where hard copy.

Feb - CI -	DIS G	.06	(−0.40 vs. 0.39)
(7/9)	NDIS G	.00	(−0.40 vs. 0.35)
	NDIS B	.05	(−0.36 vs. 0.11)
	NDIS T	.01	(−0.37 vs. −0.03)
	TOT G	.00	(−0.41 vs. 0.30)
	TOT B	.12	(−0.34 vs. −0.07)
	TOT T	.10	(−0.35 vs. −0.13)
Feb - CO -	DIS G	.17	(−0.38 vs. −0.01)
(6/9)	NDIS G	.00	(−0.36 vs. −0.41)
	NDIS B	.07	(−0.32 vs. 0.22)
	NDIS T	.05	(−0.31 vs. −0.01)
	TOT G	.01	(−0.35 vs. 0.30)
	TOT B	.20	(−0.29 vs. −0.02)

b) Increase in referral/placement ratios for good jobs less with hard copy.

Feb - CI -	DIS G	.14	(3.25 vs. 0.47)
(5/9)	NDIS G	.03	(2.75 vs. −0.94)
	NDIS B	.20	(1.64 vs. 0.29)

	NDIS	T	.19	(1.94 vs. 0.64)
	TOT	G	.03	(3.02 vs. −0.79)
Feb - CO -	NDIS	G	.07	(1.53 vs. −1.06)
(2/9)	TOT	G	.04	(1.61 vs. −0.83)

			Significance Level	Base Level for This Variable
Mar - CI -	DIS	G	.04	(3.77 vs. −0.62)
(3/9)	NDIS	G	.09	(1.54 vs. 0.09)
	TOT	G	.04	(1.60 vs. −0.16)
Mar - CO -	DIS	G	.05	(2.60 vs. −0.37)
(3/9)	NDIS	G	.01	(1.61 vs. −1.02)
	TOT	G	.01	(1.66 vs. −1.02)

c) Proportion of placements who are disadvantaged down more in February where hard copy.

Feb - CI -	TOT	B	.05	(0.03 vs. −0.09)
(2/3)	TOT	T	.09	(0.01 vs. −0.07)
Feb - CO -	TOT	G	.11	(0.00 vs. −0.06)
(3/3)	TOT	B	.02	(0.05 vs. −0.13)
	TOT	T	.03	(0.04 vs. −0.09)

d) Proportion of placements in good jobs up more where hard copy.

Feb - CI -	DIS	T	.02	(−0.02 vs. 0.06)
(3/3)	NDIS	T	.03	(−0.01 vs. 0.04)
	TOT	T	.00	(−0.01 vs. 0.05)
Feb - CO -	DIS	T	.08	(−0.02 vs. 0.04)
(3/3)	NDIS	T	.04	(−0.02 vs. 0.05)
	TOT	T	.01	(−0.02 vs. 0.05)
Mar - CI -	DIS	T	.14	(−0.04 vs. 0.05)
(1/3)				

e) Proportion of nondisadvantaged and total applicants placed is better where hard copy. Proportion of disadvantaged applicants placed is worse in one month where hard copy.

Feb -	NDIS	T	.12 hard	(−0.15 vs. 0.05)
	TOT	T	.18 copy	(−0.17 vs. −0.04)
	3 + TOT	T	.14 better	(−0.09 vs. −0.01)

| Mar - | DIS | T | .14 hard more | $(0.07$ vs. $-0.28)$ |
| | NDIS | T | .20 hard copy better | $(-0.12$ vs. $0.15)$ |

ORG. 10) Number of Local Offices

a) Time to fill openings declined most or rose least in cities with the greatest number of local offices.

			Significance Level
Feb - CI - (1/3)	TOT	B	.14
Feb - CO - (3/3)	TOT	B	.02
	TOT	G	.20
	TOT	T	.06
Mar - CO - (3/3)	TOT	B	.03
	TOT	G	.20
	TOT	T	.02

b) Ratio of placements to openings received fell less in cities with greatest number of local offices.

Feb - CI - (1/1)	.02
Feb - CO - (1/1)	.02
Mar - CI - (1/1)	.04

ORG. 11) Proportion of Openings Filled Same Day Received

a) Placements fell least in cities in which a high proportion of orders were filled same day received.

Total placements:

Feb - CO - (1/1)	.18
Mar - CO - (1/1)	.19

Regular placements:

Mar - CI -   .10
  (1/1)

Mar - CO -   .08
  (1/1)

ORG. 12) Change in Proportion of Openings Filled Same Day Received

a) Time to fill openings rose least or fell most in cities in which proportion of openings filled same day received rose.

			Significance Level	Base Level for This Variable
Feb - CI - (1/3)	TOT	B	.08	$(-6.98$ vs. $+0.38)$
Feb - CO - (1/3)	TOT	B	.11	$(-6.98$ vs. $+1.35)$
Mar - CI - (1/3)	TOT	T	.06	$(-4.40$ vs. $-0.32)$
Mar - CO - (1/3)	TOT	T	.05	$(-4.40$ vs. $-0.34)$

b) Placements fell least where proportion of openings filled first day rose.

Total placements:

Feb - CI - (1/1)	.04	$(- .42$ vs. $- .28)$
Feb - CO - (0/1)	.10	$(- .42$ vs. $- .53)$
Mar - CI - (1/1)	.14	$(- .24$ vs. $- .07)$
Mar - CO - (1/1)	.12	$(- .24$ vs. $- .11)$

Regular placements:

Feb - CI - (1/1)	.07	$(- .44$ vs. $- .29)$
Feb - CO - (1/1)	.09	$(- .44$ vs. $- .28)$

c) Openings received rose most or declined least in cities in which the proportion of openings filled same day received rose.

	Significance Level	Base Level for This Variable
Feb - CI - (1/1)	.13	$(- .29$ vs. $- .10)$
Mar - CI - (1/1)	.04	$(- .08$ vs. $+ .16)$
Mar - CO - (1/1)	.06	$(- .08$ vs. $+ .12)$

ORG. 13) Percentage of Referral Verification Carried Out by Referral Interviewers

a) Placement fell least or rose most in cities in which percentage verification by interviewers was high.

Feb - CI -	.06
Feb - CO -	.04
Mar - N/S, but close and in same direction	

b) Referral of nondisadvantaged and total to bad (DOT) jobs rose most or fell least in cities with high percentage verification by interviewers.

Feb - CI - (2/2)	NDIS B	.15
	TOT B	.16
Feb - CO - (2/2)	NDIS B	.00
	TOT B	.01
Mar - CI - (1/2)	NDIS B	.06
Mar - CO - (2/2)	NDIS B	.01
	TOT B	.02

c) NDIS and TOT placement rose more or fell less where high percentage verification by placement interviewers.

Feb - CI - (4/6)	NDIS G	.00
	NDIS B	.10
	NDIS T	.18
	TOT G	.02

		Significance Level
Feb - CO -	NDIS G	.02
(4/6)	NDIS B	.17
	NDIS T	.19
	TOT G	.00
Mar - CI -	NDIS B	.08
(1/6)		
Mar - CO -	NDIS G	.16
(2/6)	NIDS B	.19

d) Disadvantaged proportion of placements fell most where high percentage verification by referral interviewers.

Feb - CI -	DIS G	.16
(3/3)	DIS B	.03
	DIS T	.18
Feb - CO -	DIS G	.07
(2/3)	DIS B	.03
Mar - CO -	DIS T	.13
(1/3)		

Many other observations close to significant and all in same direction.

ORG. 14) Percentage Referral Verification by Central Telephone Unit

a) NDIS and TOT placements fell most in one month where high percentage central telephone verification.

Feb - CI -	NDIS G	.10
(6/6)	NDIS B	.08
	NDIS T	.01
	TOT G	.09
	TOT B	.04
	TOT T	.00
Feb - CO -	NDIS G	.18
(5/6)	NDIS B	.11
	NDIS T	.06
	TOT B	.10
	TOT T	.03

b) NDIS and TOT referral/placement ratios rose most where high percentage central telephone verification. This was especially true for good jobs.

Feb - CI -	NDIS G	.02
(6/6)	NDIS B	.05
	NDIS T	.01
	TOT G	.03
	TOT B	.07
	TOT T	.01

		Significance Level
Feb - CO -	NDIS G	.18
(5/6)	NDIS B	.20
	NDIS T	.13
	TOT G	.20
	TOT T	.20
Mar - CI -	NDIS G	.11
(4/6)	NDIS T	.09
	TOT G	.12
	TOT T	.17
Mar - CO -	NDIS G	.16
(2/6)	TOT G	.16

c) Openings received fell most in COMO out cities where high percentage central telephone verification.

Feb - CO -	TOT	.15
(1/1)		
Mar - CO -	TOT	.08
(1/1)		

ORG. 15) Total Percentage Referral Verification by Telephone

a) NDIS and TOT referrals rose most or fell least where high percentage telephone verification.

Feb - CI -	NDIS G	.03
(6/6)	NDIS B	.03
	NDIS T	.08
	TXT G	.04

	TOT	B	.04
	TOT	T	.16
Mar - CI -	NDIS	B	.11
(3/6)	NDIS	T	.20
	TOT	B	.15
Mar - CO -	NDIS	B	.20
(2/6)	TOT	B	.16

b) Referral/placement ratios tended to rise most where high percentage telephone verification.

Feb - CI -	DIS	B	.11
(8/9)	DIS	T	.01
	NDIS	G	.19
	NDIS	B	.16
	NDIS	T	.07
	TOT	G	.16
	TOT	B	.06
	TOT	T	.02
Feb - CO -	DIS	G	.20
(1/9)			
Mar - CI -	DIS	G	.17
(1/9)			

ORG. 16) Number of ES Placement Personnel

a) Nondisadvantaged and total regular placements fell most or rose least in cities with largest number of placement personnel.

			Significance Level
Feb - CI -	NDIS	G	.14
(4/6)	NDIS	B	.12
	NDIS	T	.16
	TOT	G	.19
Feb - CO -	NDIS	G	.11
(4/6)	NDIS	B	.08
	NDIS	T	.15
	TOT	G	.18
Mar - CI -	NDIS	G	.12
(5/6)	NDIS	B	.01

	NDIS T	.01
	TOT B	.04
	TOT T	.03
Mar - CO -	NDIS G	.09
(5/6)	NDIS B	.01
	NDIS T	.05
	TOT B	.06
	TOT T	.08

b) Disadvantaged proportion of total placements rose most or fell least in one month in cities with largest number of placement personnel.

Feb - CI -	B	.01
(2/3)	T	.02
Feb - CO -	G	.05
(3/3)	B	.00
	T	.01

c) Proportion of disadvantaged and total placements that were in "good" DOT jobs fell most in one month in cities with largest number of placement personnel.

Feb - CI -	DIS	.07
(2/2)	TOT	.08
Feb - CO -	DIS	.09
(2/2)	TOT	.09

ORG. 17) Ratio of Walk-in Referrals to Total Referrals

a) Placements in "Bad" jobs and "Total" jobs declined less where high ratio of walk-in referrals to total referrals.

		Significance Level
Feb - CO -	NDIS B	.09
(3/6)	TOT B	.05
	TOT T	.15
Mar - CI -	NDIS T	.17
(2/6)	TOT B	.20

Mar - CO -	DIS	B	.04
(6/6)	DIS	T	.19
	NDIS	B	.15
	NDIS	T	.05
	TOT	B	.05
	TOT	T	.08

Control Variables

CON. 1) Unemployment Rate

a) Five measures of unemployment were correlated with time to fill openings. The measures and the significance of the correlations are as follows:

| | Significance Levels | | | |
| | February | | March | |
	CI	CO	CI	CO
1. Absolute change in unemployment rate, coded 0, 1	.012	.024	.057	.177
2. Absolute change in unemployment rate, actual changes	.007	.013	.016	.046
3. Relative change in unemployment rate, actual changes	.042	.032	.039	.043
4. 1970 unemployment rate, actual rate	.166	NS	NS	NS
5. 1971 unemployment rate, actual rate	NS	NS	NS	NS

The mean unemployment rate change between February 1970 and February 1971 was 1.4%. A 1% change in rate was associated with an inverse 6.76 day change in time to fill openings.

The mean unemployment rate change between March 1970 and March 1971 was 1.2%. A 1% change in rate was associated with an inverse 4.37 day change in time to fill openings.

Since the actual decrease in average time to fill openings was less than the decrease associated with the actual unemployment rate changes, we infer that time to fill openings would have risen had unemployment remained stable.

b) Time to Fill Jobs vs. Occupational Mix.

	1970		1971	
	Feb.	Mar.	Feb.	Mar.
Mean time good jobs, and good job proportion of all jobs	NS	.17	NS	NS
Mean time bad jobs, and bad job proportion of all jobs	NS	NS	NS	.03
Mean time all jobs, and good job proportion of all jobs	.14	.09	NS	NS
Mean time all jobs, and bad job proportion of all jobs	NS	NS	NS	.11

CON. 2) SMSA Population

a) Time to fill openings declined most or rose least in cities with largest populations.

			Significance Level
Feb - CI -	TOT	G	.04
(3/3)	TOT	B	.17
	TOT	T	.04
Feb - CO -	TOT	G	.09
(2/3)	TOT	T	.03
Mar - CI -	TOT	G	.09
(3/3)	TOT	B	.11
	TOT	T	.09
Mar - CO -	TOT	G	.11
(3/3)	TOT	B	.12
	TOT	T	.10

b) Regular placements fell most in cities with largest populations.

February

CI - Table VII	TOT	T	.05
CI - Table I	NDIS	G	.16
(2/10)			
CO - Table VII	TOT	T	.05
CO - Table I	NDIS	G	.08
(4/10)	NDIS	T	.16
	TOT	G	.11

March

CI - Table VII	TOT	T	.19
CI - Table I	DIS	B	.17
(9/10)	DIS	T	.15
	NDIS	G	.05
	NDIS	B	.01
	NDIS	T	.02
	TOT	G	.08
	TOT	B	.02
	TOT	T	.02
CO - Table VII	TOT	T	.08
CO - Table I	NDIS	G	.06
(7/10)	NDIS	B	.11
	NDIS	T	.03
	TOT	G	.06
	TOT	B	.03
	TOT	T	.03

c) Openings received declined most in one month in cities with largest populations.

Mar - CI -	.15
(1/1)	
Mar - CO -	.05
(1/1)	

d) Ratio of placements to openings received increased most in one month in cities with largest populations.

Mar - CI -	.03
(1/1)	
Mar - CO -	.03
(1/1)	

CON. 3) Start-up Date, Calculated As Number of Months after January 1970

This variable was discarded from the analysis, due to insufficient variation in start-up month. Because nearly all Job Banks in the sample started in June, very great weight accrues to Job Banks started in other months. Hence, a relationship existing in a single city can have a great effect on the entire sample.

Even though *statistically* significant relationships are obtained in such circumstances, the outcome does not have *practical* significance.

Appendix 3: National Office Communications to the State Agencies

In reply refer
to MEHSM

U.S. DEPARTMENT OF LABOR
Manpower Administration
Washington, D.C. 20210

Training and Employment Service
Program Letter No. 2525
November 14, 1969

TO: ALL STATE EMPLOYMENT SECURITY AGENCIES

SUBJECT: Expansion of the Job Bank Concept

REFERENCES: None

PURPOSE: To provide information on the computer-assisted system of job order development, distribution, and control initiated by the Maryland agency and usually referred to as the Job Bank.

The Baltimore Job Bank became fully operational in May 1968. As a result HRD placements more than doubled, increasing from less than 20 percent to more than 50 percent of total placements made in the geographic area served by the Job Bank. The Job Bank concept is being given high priority by the Manpower Administration. Job Banks are already operational in Portland, Oregon; St. Louis, Missouri; Chicago, Illinois; Seattle, Washington; Washington, D.C.; and Hartford, Connecticut; and close to operational in Atlanta, Georgia and Pittsburgh, Pennsylvania.

The system developed by the Maryland agency is relatively simple. It does not use the computer to do actual matching of people and jobs, but simply provides all counselors and placement interviewers in the Employment Service and 18 cooperating agencies in the Baltimore metropolitan area with a daily listing of job openings in the area listed with the Employment Service or these agencies. In addition to many other indirect values discussed below, this system has these basic operating advantages: (1) it provides for excellent distribution of job openings to employment service staff and personnel of cooperating agencies;

139

(2) it substantially reduces excessive referrals of workers to employers; and (3) it substantially reduces excessive job solicitation visits to employers.

General Operation of the Baltimore Job Bank

Each morning about 50 sets of the Job Bank book are distributed to desks in the Baltimore central local office and to 15 or more outreach stations at key points in the metropolitan area. Desk space in the central office is made available to cooperating community agencies. The book itself, duplicated from the original computer fanfold printout, normally contains about 6,000 current job openings arranged in DOT sequence. Also listed are training slots, apprenticeship openings, and other types of job orders, including noncontract jobs from the National Alliance of Businessmen.

Referrals are monitored and kept within stated limits by a telephone control unit which approves or denies interviewers' requests to refer applicants, depending upon the status of the order.

At the close of business, information on the day's operation, including referrals, cancelled or new orders, or changes in listed orders, are collected and fed to the computer. Information on hires and related facts are verified by mail and telephone and keypunched for overnight input into the computer. New openings received during the day are keypunched after close of business along with other transactions. Provision is made for exposing new openings to applicants on the day they are received.

Job Bank Potential

The Job Bank concept holds great potential for improving the management and delivery of manpower services. The installation of a Job Bank in a metropolitan area can be a major step toward making the Employment Service the hub of the manpower delivery system in the community. Some of the advantages of the system as evidenced in Baltimore are:

1. Elimination of competition among manpower agencies, thereby avoiding multiple and duplicative job solicitations.

2. Decentralization of staff into neighborhoods where the target population lives, without loss of control and quality supervision of that staff.

3. Increase in referrals and placements of disadvantaged job seekers, while maintaining volume of total placements.

4. Data derived from a Job Bank will assist in more effective planning, redirection, and coordination of employer relations and job development efforts.

5. An improved system of management and supervisory controls over volume and quality of order-taking, selection, referral, and verification by computer printouts of definitive data on qualitative and quantitative bases, on individual interviewers, and office or unit performance on a daily, weekly, or monthly basis.

6. Establishment of a source of current information about jobs and job opportunities for use in job market information, manpower planning, planning for MDTA and vocational education, CAMPS, etc.

7. An improved level of community acceptance from employers, job seekers, and the political, social, and economic power structure of the community.

8. Acceptance of Employment Service assistance by inner-city or disadvantaged populations.

9. Creative use of Community Aides in outreach activities.

10. Increase in public relations interest and support for employment service programs in all news media—radio, TV, and newspapers.

11. Substantial improvement in UI operations due to current and specific job market information made available to interviewers to assist them in determining eligibility and providing assistance to claimants in their efforts to find work.

National Job Bank Plans

Publicity on Job Banks has been considerable. Most important, the President has publicly stated his interest in a "National Computer Job Bank," and Title IV of the Administration's proposed "Manpower Training Act of 1969" concerns Job Bank development. Attachment 1 contains a list of the cities scheduled for fiscal year 1970 Job Bank operations as of September 30, 1969.

Using the Baltimore design, with some modification to meet special local area needs, a Job Bank can be installed with at least second-generation ADP equipment and a minimum of personnel for machine operations. All other staff requirements can be met through redirection of employment service personnel. More specific information on planning for establishment of a Job Bank is included in the outline in attachment 2. Determination of the job order form content and format, consistent with the data requirements of ESARS, in key-punchable or other data convertible form, is basic to the design of the system and should be given first priority in employment service job bank planning.

A manual Job Bank system, not requiring the use of ADP equipment, has been developed in Hartford, Connecticut. It appears to be feasible for cities of smaller size where it is desired to employ the Job Bank concept, but where ADP equipment is not available.

Subsequent plans envision moving from the Job Bank concept to the job matching concept nationally. The experimental efforts involved in this national development program will be described in a forthcoming program letter.

In planning a Job Bank installation, the procedure should insure that veterans are given preference in referral to all job openings. A field communication is planned which will establish a veterans' employment unit as one means of assuring this preference.

Regional offices will communicate shortly with State agencies concerned, if they have not already done so, on Job Bank operations. Regional and national office assistance is available.

RESCISSIONS: None

> Malcolm R. Lovell, Jr.
> Deputy Assistant Secretary
> for Manpower and
> Manpower Administrator

Attachments (2)
1. Job Bank Cities, Fiscal Year 1970
2. Planning Considerations for Establishing a Job Bank

In reply refer
to MSOI

U.S. DEPARTMENT OF LABOR
Manpower Administration
Washington, D.C. 20210

General Administration Letter No. 1353
January 9, 1970

TO: ALL STATE EMPLOYMENT SECURITY AGENCIES

SUBJECT: Job Bank Operations Review and Job Bank Area Activities
                Requirements for Proposed and On-going Job Banks

REFERENCES: TESPL 2525

PURPOSE: To provide instructions for collection and submittal of statistical information on Job Bank operations and ES activities of the Job Bank area.

The attached Job Bank Operations Review requirements are designed to provide data on the operations of Job Banks. The data will be used by State agencies and the MA national office in assessing the performance of Job Banks. The Job Bank Operations Review is designed to help determine if the various Job Banks are meeting the goals of the program; i.e., improved service to the disadvantaged and a more effective placement system. The method used is to collect data from Job Bank areas for several months prior to the implementation of the Job Bank, and for one year after implementation. Comparison of before and after data from the various areas will help assess the impact of the program. The data collected after implementation will also be useful as pre-Job Matching System data as an aid for assessing the effectiveness of the Job Matching System vis-à-vis the Job Bank system.

All operating Job Banks and all areas scheduled for the implementation of a Job Bank in fiscal year 1970 are required to collect specified data each month beginning with February 1970, and continuing through 12 complete months of the operation of each bank. Each month, data required for the Job Bank Operations Review (see attached table formats I-VI should be prepared and submitted in ES-201 envelopes for each area in which a Job Bank has been operational for two or more complete calendar months.

Areas scheduled to implement a Job Bank are required to collect information each month, (Pre-Job Bank data) beginning with February 1970, to the first complete month of operation, using the attached instructions for the Pre-Job Bank Operations Review Order Activity and the Referral Outcome Cards (see attachment 1). If a Job Bank begins operation in the middle of a month, Pre-Job Bank data collection should be continued through the end of that month. Beginning with the first complete month of operation of the automated system, the data for Tables I through VI should be collected directly from the system. Thereafter the pre-Job Bank cards will no longer be used. Pre-Job Bank data should be held and submitted with the initial Job Bank Operations Review (JBOR) which is due in the MA national office the 20th of the month following the second complete calendar month after the implementation of the Job Bank. Subsequent JBOR's are due the 20th of the month following the month to which the data relate. Three sets of all tables should be submitted to the MA national office and one set to the appropriate regional office.

To illustrate the timing, if a Job Bank began operation in December 1969, or before, February data should be submitted by March 20, 1970. However, if a Job Bank begins in mid-March, with its first complete month of operation being April, data for the pre-Job Bank period and the first two completed months of operation should be submitted by June 20, 1970; i.e., separate data for the months of February through May 1970 would be submitted.

The collection of JBOR data and the production of Tables I-VI will be accomplished by the automated system after a Job Bank is operational. Therefore, the main cost of the JBOR is incurred in collecting the pre-Job Bank data. State agencies are encouraged to include a budget item for collecting the pre-Job Bank data in their Supplemental Budget Request (SBR).

Each State agency should reproduce its own supply of transmittal sheets and table VII. (See attachment 2 for formats). Tables I-VI should be generated as computer output and therefore need not be reproduced. Instructions for obtaining data for the JBOR (Tables I-VI) are contained in attachment 1. Instructions for Preparation of Transmittal Sheets, JBOR, Tables I-VI, and Table VII, Job Bank Area Activities, are contained in attachment 2.

The Job Bank Operations Review requirements have been approved by the Bureau of the Budget in accordance with the Federal Reports Act of 1942.

Malcolm R. Lovell, Jr.
Deputy Assistant Secretary
for Manpower and
Manpower Administrator

Attachments (2)
1. Instructions for Obtaining Data
   for the Job Bank Operations Review
2. Instructions for Preparation and
   Submittal of Job Bank Operations
   Review Tables I-VI and Table VII,
   Job Bank Area Activities

In reply refer
to MEEM

U.S. DEPARTMENT OF LABOR
Manpower Administration
Washington, D.C. 20210

Training and Employment Service
Program Letter No. 2726
April 21, 1972

TO: ALL STATE EMPLOYMENT SECURITY AGENCIES

SUBJECT: Preliminary Job Bank Finding; Implications for Operations
and Organization

PURPOSE: To transmit recommendations for improving Job Bank operations

Two formal evaluations of Job Bank operations and organization are currently underway by two contractors. Some preliminary results have been made available from both studies. These results, particularly those from the University of Wisconsin project, coupled with our own findings based on study of "Job Bank Operational Review" (JBOR) data, indicate that several improvements in the operations of Job Bank can be made at this time. State agencies which have not already done so, are urged to implement the following recommendations in all Job Banks:

1. *Specialization.*

   Order taking should be specialized and organized by employer or industry. The referral function should be organized on an occupational basis. In most Job Banks which operate on a specialized basis, specialization occurs in this way. The findings do not imply, however, that order taking and referral functions should be merged. They simply mean that within order taking and within referral, specialization should exist. Specialization allows the knowledge accumulated by individual interviewers about firms and occupations to be used more effectively by the Job Bank staff.

2. *Employer Relations.*

   State agencies have been encouraged to strengthen their employer relations programs within the past year. Studies have shown that Job Banks located in cities with a strong employer relations program attract more and better job openings than those with a relatively weak program.

3. *Interviewer Access.*

Each interviewer should have his own Job Bank book or display device. Easy access to job listings is a prerequisite for providing adequate, timely service for applicants.

4. *First Day Service.*

Procedures for first day referral should be examined with a view to providing service on a job order the day it is received. These procedures should include selective advance distribution of orders to expedite first day referral. For example, the veterans units should receive and work on orders immediately after they are received. Evidence indicates that Job Bank in itself does not decrease the overall time required to fill job orders. Procedures which stress first day referral and prompt verification of referrals are a necessary step toward reducing the time required to fill openings.

5. *Verification.*

Early experience with the use of an automatic mailer proved to be too slow in verifying the results of referrals. Telephone verification saves job openings from being lost and increases employer satisfaction. Verification of referrals within the shortest practical time (24 hours to a maximum of 3 days) is essential to the continued effectiveness of the system.

It is anticipated that additional information based on further analysis will be forthcoming over the next few months. The above recommendations are based on convincing evidence, however, and it is very likely that they will be confirmed by additional study. Because of the importance of reversing the decline in placement and of providing more efficient and effective placement service to applicants and employers, these recommendations are being issued now so immediate action can be taken.

PAUL J. FASSER, JR.
Deputy Assistant Secretary
for Manpower and
Manpower Administrator

Appendix 4: Questionnaire Used to Collect Data on the Job Bank Design Configurations

JOB BANK OPERATIONS FLOW STUDY

City _____   Date form completed _____

Region _____   Regional Office staff _____
                                member completing form _____

Instructions

1. Respond in relation to the procedures and organizational structure as they presently exist. A forthcoming change notice to GAL 1353 will describe the method for reporting changes in these procedures and structures.
2. If a question is not applicable, enter NA in the answer space. If it is not clear from other answers why the question is not applicable, please explain.

Order Taking: If order taking is centralized answer 1 and 2
If order taking is not centralized answer 3

1.a. How many full-time equivalent persons work as order takers in central order-taking? _15_
 b. What percent of these persons have worked previously as ES interviewers? _100%_
 c. Describe the nature and duration of training given to those order takers who had no previous experience as order takers. _NA_
 d. What percent of the order takers working in central order taking also act as Employer Relations Representatives? _-0-_
 e. What percent of the job orders are being taken directly from employers by central order-taking? _92.5%_
 f. What percent are being taken by community agencies? _½%_
 g. What percent are being taken by individual ES interviewers not part of a central order-taking unit? _3%_
 h. What percent are being taken by other means? (E.g., ERR, Counselors etc.) _4%_
 i. Comments _____
2.a. In what ways, if any, do the members of central order taking specialize? (Check one or more.)

none   _X_
occupationally   _____

147

industrially   _____

first letter of firm name   _____

OTHER (specify)   _____

b. If specialized, describe the various specialties (e.g., professional-technical, commercial, blue collar, and service work; or A – F, G – Q, R – Z). __NA__

_____

c. Comments (particularly for this question, it is important to note any changes planned for future dates). _____

_____

3.a. Estimate total percentage of interviewer time devoted to order taking? __NA_____

b. How many equivalent positions does this represent? _____

c. What percent of the job orders are being taken directly by community agencies? _____

d. What percent are being taken by other means? (E.g., ERR, Counselors etc.) _____

e. Comments _____

_____

_____

Interviewing

4.a. In what way, if any, do the members of the referral units specialize? (Check one or more.)

none   ___X_____

occupationally   _____

industrially   _____

other (Please specify.)   _____

b. If specialized, describe the various specialty classes (e.g., professional-technical, commercial, blue-collar, and service work).

__NA_____

_____

_____

c. Comments _____

_____

_____

5.a. What is the standard or prescribed number of referrals allowed per opening when the employer does not specify a desired number of openings? __Three__

b. Give details if a different number is allowed in different occupations or circumstances. _____
_____

c. Comments _____

Verification

6.a. *Orders*

i. What proportion is verified by a central unit? __97%_____
Method used: Mail __X__ Phone __X__ Other (specify) _____

ii. What proportion is verified by interviewer? __½%_____
Method used: Mail _____ Phone _____ Other (specify) _____

iii. What proportion is verified by other means? __2-5% by ERR's_____

6.b. *Referrals*

i. How many full-time equivalent positions work as verifiers in central referral-verification unit? __15_____

ii. What proportion of verification is accomplished by:
a. "speedy mailer" referral result cards? __76%_____
b. referring interviewer using mail __-0-_____
phone __½__ Other (specify) _____
c. other means __21% verification unit phone ERR unit 2.5%_____
d. never verified _____

iii. Please indicate the timing sequence used, e.g., "phone calls within two days after each referral" __Employer contacted by phone 9 days after referral if "speedy mailer" not returned_____

iv. Please describe present or proposed changes to verification method and the reason for the change _____
__48 hr., telephone verification—all orders_____

v. Comments _____
_____
_____

6.c. Do the same individuals usually do order verification and referral verification? __yes__. If not, identify different units involved _____
_____

d. Comments _____
_____
_____

Output

7.a. What is the output mode? hard copy book __X__ micro-film _____
microfishe_____

b. In what ways is the output indexed? (check one or more)

DOT-code	X
Duration (temporary)	
Location	
Age of order	
Part-time	
Employer	
Industry	
Other (Please specify)	

c. Comments _Training opportunities, NAB-JOBS, AIC, and summer jobs listed separately by DOT code_

Resource allocation

8.a. Indicate the number of locations of each type to which JB books or viewers are distributed.

conventional local offices	10	UI offices	10
community agencies	30	CEP offices	1
small outreach offices	5	Other (Please specify)	
		WIN	1

b. In the offices included in the Job Bank, how many Employment Service full-time equivalent persons are involved in placement-related activities such as order-taking, interviewing, employer relations, and counseling, as distinct from reporting or industrial service.
290

c. What is the ratio of JB books or viewers to interviewers? one to three

d. What is the ratio of JB books or viewers to counselors? one to four

e. Of these persons, how many full-time equivalent persons work in multi-service centers or other offices staffed partly by other than Employment Service personnel (including CEP)? 42

f. Of the ES persons reported in b., how many full-time equivalent persons work in ES offices located in poverty areas? 270

g. Of the persons reported in b., how many full-time equivalent persons work as Employer Relations Representatives, or similar capacities?
46

h. What percent of the total ERR-obtained information is directed to each of the following destinations?

employer file	100%	interviewers	20%
statistical reporting file	25%	general administrative use	100%
non-interviewing order takers	100%	others (please specify)	

i. Comments _____
    _____
    _____

9.a. List the community agencies which participate in the Job Bank.

(13) Hartrandt Corp – 2   (14) Temple Community Health Center – 2

1 OCI   6 locations   6 NYC
2 BVR   2 locations   7 Model Cities – 2
3 JEVS   8 Phila. Urban League
4 Mayors Utilization   9 Smith, Kline & French
      Commission   2   10 Cassa Del. Carman
5 Commission on Human   11 Negro Trade Council
      Relations   12 Phila. Tutorial

b. How many of these agencies deal principally with the disadvantaged?
    Eighteen _____
c. How many of those agencies dealing principally with the disadvantaged
    have the Job Bank book available on their own premises? Eighteen _____
d. Comments Penna. agency personnel are not stationed at community
    stations. There is a waiting list of approximately 15 community agencies
    waiting to participate in the Job Bank. _____

10.a. *What means* were used to advertise the presence of the Job Bank to the
       community, employers, potential applicants, and community agencies, and
       how strenuously were the associated efforts? (Check appropriate boxes.)

	Considerable	Moderate	Minimal	Nonexistent
ERR's explained JB to all major market employers	X			
Explanatory Mailing to all employers	X			
TV, radio, newspaper	X			
Meeting with community agencies	X			
Others (Please specify)				
Meetings with employer, labor and civic organizations	X			

11.a. What types of jobs are excluded from the Job Bank? (Check one or more)

casual	X
domestic	

professional   _____
first-day placements   _____
other (please specify)   _____

b. Circle types of jobs also excluded from Job Bank Operation Review Tables.

c. Comments First-day placements are put into the system but do not appear in the book.

Notes

Notes

Chapter 1
Introduction and Overview

1. Studies of manpower programs have usually been conducted retrospectively by persons outside the organization responsible for operating the programs. Usually, the researchers had to use whatever data were available and had little impact on the character or quality of the data. In the present study, desired performance data were specified in advance, collected, analyzed, and reported back to program administrators by persons closely associated with the operating program. This situation offered a rare opportunity and, in fact, made the research reported here possible.

2. For a summary of recent federal efforts in this regard, see U.S. President, MANPOWER REPORT OF THE PRESIDENT, 1972 (Washington, D.C.: GPO, 1972), pp. 141-45.

3. Charles C. Holt, et al., THE UNEMPLOYMENT-INFLATION DILEMMA: A MANPOWER SOLUTION, (Washington, D.C.: The Urban Institute, 1971).

4. See, for example, Joseph C. Ullman and David P. Taylor, "The Information System in Changing Labor Markets," PROCEEDINGS OF THE EIGHTEENTH ANNUAL MEETING (Madison, Wisconsin: IRRA, 1966), pp. 276-89.

5. Although it is sometimes argued that some new agency, rather than the Employment Service, could better serve the placement role associated with an income-maintenance program, the arguments in favor of using the Employment Service seem overwhelming. For a discussion of this issue, see Stanley H. Ruttenberg and Jocelyn Gutchess. THE FEDERAL-STATE EMPLOYMENT SERVICE: A CRITIQUE (Baltimore: Johns Hopkins Press, 1970), pp. 69-72.

6. The research also examined the extent to which Job Banks are achieving two additional goals: first, to maintain or increase the overall volume of Employment Service activity; and second, to provide more flexible, rapid, and direct manpower services to employers and workers. The present study did not examine the degree of achievement of several other goals related to internal management rather than labor-market operations.

7. Ruttenberg and Gutchess, EMPLOYMENT SERVICE, p. 103.

8. Glen G. Cain and Robinson G. Hollister, "The Methodology of Evaluating Social Action Program," in PUBLIC-PRIVATE MANPOWER POLICIES, Arnold R. Weber, et al., eds., Industrial Relations Research Association, 1969, pp. 28-29.

Chapter 2
Job Banks and the Design of the
Job Bank Study

1. U.S. President, MANPOWER REPORT OF THE PRESIDENT, 1971 (Washington, D.C.: GPO, 1971), p. 179.

2. Excerpted from "Nixon on the Issues."

3. Arnold R. Weber, "Introduction," in PUBLIC-PRIVATE MANPOWER POLICIES, Arnold R. Weber, et al., eds., Industrial Relations Research Association, 1969, pp. 2-3.

4. This section is taken from George P. Huber and Joseph C. Ullman, "Computer Job Matching—How and How Well," MANPOWER 2, no. 11, November 1970.

5. In Hartford, multiple copies of each job order were produced and distributed to the various Employment Service offices. Central telephone control was exercised over referrals. However, there was no use at all made of the computer. Hence, the Hartford operation was actually a quasi-Job Bank initially.

6. Given that the fifty-six city goal had not been announced until October 1969, the implementation of this many Job Banks in such a short period of time was considered a major achievement within the Department of Labor.

7. The discussion is based on the Manpower Administration document, "Phased Implementation Progression for Computer-Assisted Manpower Operations Network," May 1, 1970.

8. For an indication of the nature of the computational and psychometric technology that can be brought to bear on the man-job matching problem, see G. Huber and C. Falkner, "Computer Based Man-Job Matching Systems: Current Practice and Applicable Research," SOCIO-ECONOMIC PLANNING SCIENCES 3, no. 3, December 1969; G. Huber, R. Daneshgar, and D. Ford, "An Empirical Comparison of Five Utility Models for Predicting Job Preference," ORGANIZA-TIONAL BEHAVIOR AND HUMAN PERFORMANCE 6, no. 3, May 1971; and D. Ford, G. Huber and D. Gustafson, "Predicting Job Choices with Models that Contain Subjective Probability Judgments: An Empirical Comparison of Five Models." ORGANIZATIONAL BEHAVIOR AND HUMAN PERFORMANCE 7, no. 3, June 1972.

9. Announced and described in GAL 1463, dated May 17, 1972.

10. For a discussion of these problems, see Huber and Ullman, "Computer Job Matching," pp. 2-6.

Chapter 3
Findings Concerning the Performance and
Design of Local Job Banks

1. The earlier papers were (1) "The Relation between Job Bank Organization and the Skill Mix of Openings Received," March 1971; (2) "An Interim

Analysis of Job Bank Performance Data," November 1971; (3) "Improving the Operation of Local Job Banks," December 1971; and (4) "Improving the Operation of Local Job Banks: A Further Look," March 1972.

2. These previously conducted studies were reported in the following papers: (1) "Preliminary Job Bank Data from Six Cities," March 1970; (2) "Report on Job Bank Interview Study," April 1970; and (3) "Employer Reactions to the Job Bank: A Report on Interviews in Four Cities," May 1971.

3. Phased Implementation Plan is the shorthand title for the overall plan to introduce computer technology to Public Employment Service operations. The plan calls for a series of accretive steps, based on experience with early systems and experimentation. The full plan is discussed in detail in "Phased Implementation Progression for Computer-Assisted Manpower Operations Network," written by USTES staff and dated May 1970.

4. These recommendations are based solely on what appears to be most effective in existing Job Banks. We have not speculated about possible variations of existing attributes, because our task was not to generate new solutions. Similarly, our assessment of existing options is based entirely on operational considerations, and not on such other factors as dollar cost or social effects.

5. Virtually all order-taker specialization in sample cities is by employer whereas referral unit specialization is nearly always by occupation.

6. Even though there are eight recommendations, only six specific design features are proposed.

7. This discussion in no way detracts from or diminishes the validity of our recommendations. None of our recommendations are based on as few as three cities, because the corresponding analyses were made one attribute at a time and thus included the large number of cities that manifested that particular attribute.

8. "An Evaluation of Results and Effectiveness of Job Banks," Ultrasystems, Incorporated, Newport Beach, California, March 1972. This study was conducted under Contract Number 83-06-72-01 with the Office of Policy, Evaluation and Research, Manpower Administration.

9. The comparison cities were the larger cities that did not have Job Banks. Since Job Banks were, for the most part, installed in the more populous SMSAs, the comparison cities were more like Job Bank cities than were any other non-Job Bank cities, but were still unlike them in the sense of being smaller. Also, after eliminating the COMO cities, the comparison cities were found to have a higher average base (1970) unemployment rate than did the Job Bank cities, although the average *change* in unemployment over the study period was similar in the two sets of cities. *All of our conclusions with respect to the goal achievement of local Job Banks takes the above facts into account.* Stepwise multiple regression, a statistical technique that allowed for study of the effect of Job Bank after the effect of population and unemployment had been accounted for, provided us this capability. Whether using this technique, or ignoring the effects of population and unemployment, or matching the two sets of cities for population by eliminating the more populous of the Job Bank cities and the less populous of the Comparison cities, the results and conclusions were the same.

10. At the June 26 meeting at which this report was discussed, an administrator pointed out that Job Banks increase the intensiveness of information available to those applicants seeing interviewers who did not record the job order. That is to say, under the non-Job Bank system job orders are written in a very sketchy manner, primarily to aid the recall of the interviewer order taker, while in a Job Bank, interviewers must write down more detailed information for the sake of their colleagues. This more complete write-up results in more intensive information for every interviewer than would have been available under the previous system. The net effect of this increase in intensiveness and the possible decreases described here is unclear, but our statement that intensiveness is unaffected is incorrect.

11. See Albert E. Rees, "Information Networks in Labor Markets," AMERICAN ECONOMIC REVIEW May 1966, pp. 559-66.

12. It should be pointed out that Job Banks only affect the portion of the labor market served by the Public Employment Service—perhaps 10 percent of all placements, but perhaps a higher proportion of placements of unemployed persons. It is the Employment Service proportion of the latter kind of placement that determines the potential impact of Job Banks on frictional unemployment.

13. This conclusion of course applies only within the range of our data. It is certain that the average time to fill an opening for a company president is larger than the comparable time for a janitor opening. However, the occupational mix among Employment Service cities in our sample, and between months, did not vary enough to reveal such a relationship.

14. At the June 26 meeting, an administrator pointed out that Job Banks are necessary to operate the Job Information Service (JIS), an applicant self-service system, and that this clearly increases the flexibility and directness of service to applicants where JIS is a part of the ES system.

Chapter 4
Findings Concerning the Effect of Feedback on Program Administration and Administrators

1. P.M. Blau, THE DYNAMICS OF BUREAUCRACY. Chicago: University of Chicago Press, 1955.

2. R.S. Weiss and M. Rein, "The Evaluation of Broad Aim Programs: Experimental Design, Its Difficulties, and an Alternative," ADMINISTRATIVE SCIENCE QUARTERLY 15, no. 1, March 1970, pp. 97-109.

3. Weiss and Rein (1970), ibid.

4. FAP was the acronym for Family Assistance Plan, the welfare reform proposal being pushed by the Nixon administration at this time.

5. Studies are indicated by headings shown in quotation marks. If anyone other than the present researchers were primarily responsible for producing the

report, this is indicated in parentheses after the heading. If no parenthetical listing occurs, the present researchers were primarily responsible for the report.

6. An examination of monthly data revealed one month (July 1968) in which disadvantaged placements were as much as 55% of total placements.

7. At this luncheon meeting, MLA opened by saying, "I think evaluation should tell us how to make programs work, not just that programs are no good." This observation led us to focus more on Job Bank design than had been true to that point. Henceforth, we attempted to combine positive proposals for improving Job Bank design with feedback concerning overall performance, particularly when the overall performance data were not positive.

8. "Preliminary Job Bank Data from Six Cities," dated March 13, 1970. The report, although unsigned was prepared by the present researchers while on the staff of LLA.

9. The report developed from this study, from which this section is taken is titled "Report on Job Bank Interview Study," undated. The introduction to the report notes that the present authors designed and supervised the interview study.

10. This decision was actually part of the larger decision made at this time to accept the philosophy and tentative schedule put forth in the PIP staff paper. This was a key decision from the point of view of Job Banks, as PIP emphasized relying on Job Banks during the several-year period in which more sophisticated systems were being developed. Another possible strategy would have been to push for earlier implementation of the more sophisticated systems.

11. Recommendations 6 and 7 concerning number of local offices and procedures for verifying referrals were not presented until the March 24, 1972 meeting.

12. This Program Letter, TESPL No. 2726, dated April 21, 1972, is reproduced in Appendix 3.

13. Selecting program goals is clearly not an entirely objective matter. Although the Ultrasystems researchers inferred goals in part from the same March 18, 1969 memorandum used by us for inferring goals, Ultrasystems chose an entirely different set of goals as indicated here. Further inquiry revealed at least part of the reason for this difference. Ultrasystems determined goals at least partly by asking LLA's staff what the goals of the Job Bank Program were, in discussions occurring after first fifty-five Job Banks were in operation.

14. H.E. Freeman and C.C. Sherwood, "Research in Large-Scale Intervention Programs," THE JOURNAL OF SOCIAL ISSUES 21, no. 1, January 1965, pp. 11-28.

15. Weiss and Rein (1970), "Evaluation."

16. W.J. Gore, ADMINISTRATIVE DECISION-MAKING: AN HEURISTIC MODEL (New York: Wiley, 1964).

17. H.C. Shulberg and F. Baker, "Program Evaluation Models and the Implementation of Research Findings," AMERICAN JOURNAL OF PUBLIC HEALTH 58, 1968.

18. Thomas P. Ference, "Organizational Communications Systems and the Decision Process." MANAGEMENT SCIENCE 17, no. 2, October 1970.

19. G. Pitz, "An Inertia Effect (Resistance) in the Revision of Opinion." CANADIAN JOURNAL OF PSYCHOLOGY 23, no. 1, 1969.

20. Edward C. Webster, DECISION-MAKING IN THE EMPLOYMENT INTERVIEW, Montreal Industrial Relations Centre, McGill University, 1964.

21. Donald T. Campbell, "Considering the Case against Experimental Evaluations of Social Innovations." ADMINISTRATIVE SCIENCE QUARTERLY, 15, no. 1, March 1970.

22. A. Downs, INSIDE BUREAUCRACY (Boston: Little Brown & Co., 1967), p. 272.

23. Ruttenberg and Gutchess, EMPLOYMENT SERVICE, p. 63.

24. THE WALL STREET JOURNAL, December 8, 1970.

25. Reported in Bureau of National Affairs "Manpower Information Service," p. 466, June 21, 1972.

26. J.D. Thompson, ORGANIZATIONS IN ACTION, New York: McGraw-Hill, 1967.

27. Downs (1965), BUREAUCRACY.

28. W.H. Read, "Upward Communications in Industrial Hierarchies," HUMAN RELATIONS 15, 1962.

29. S. Rosen and A. Tesser, "On the Reluctance to Communicate Undesirable Information: The MUM Effect," SOCIOMETRY 33, 1970, pp. 253-63.

Chapter 5
Concluding Observations

1. Freeman and Sherwood (1965), "Intervention Programs."

2. Weiss and Rein (1970), "Evaluation."

3. M.B. Miles, H.A. Hornstein, D.M. Callahan, P.H. Calder, and R.S. Schiavo, "The Consequences of Survey Feedback: Theory and Evaluation," In W.G. Bennes, K.D. Benne, and R. Chin (eds.), THE PLANNING OF CHANGE, New York: Holt, Rinehart and Winston, 1969.

4. H.C. Shulberg and F. Baker, "Program Evaluation Models and the Implementation of Research Findings," AMERICAN JOURNAL OF PUBLIC HEALTH 58, 1968, pp. 1248-55.

5. For a very interesting documentation of this point, see W.J. Gore, ADMINISTRATIVE DECISION-MAKING.

6. Shulberg and Baker state the same points as follows, "It is suggested that feedback can be enhanced by the design of evaluation procedures which more appropriately fit the scheduled decision-making needs of an organization, and which have data available at a time when they can be used for planning." Shulberg and Baker (1968), "Program Evaluation Models."

7. The next section contains a discussion relating this item to our findings.

8. If the feedback regarded as evaluative of policy is negative, it tends not to be communicated as quickly or as expansively as if it is positive. Also, of course if any feedback is congruent with policy, it is more likely to be acted upon than merely communicated. Thus it may be that the location of the key administrator is not only a function of the subject of the feedback but also the valence of the feedback.

Appendix 1
Design and Methodology of the Research

1. For an articulate discussion of this phenomenon, see A. Downs, INSIDE BUREAUCRACY (Boston: Little Brown & Co., 1967), pp. 212-16.

2. Codified on October 20, 1969 in a memorandum from ASM(1) to the Manpower Administrator.

3. In April of 1971 the researchers wrote to the officials involved in handling the JBOR data, indicating to them that considerably less data was being received than had been expected. We are unsure what effect this communication had on the officials but believe it had little effect on the number of reports received.

4. A source close to the R&R Committee subsequently confirmed that the Committee position on JBOR was affected by the organizational manner in which JBOR was designed and implemented.

5. Ruttenberg and Gutchess, EMPLOYMENT SERVICE, p. 87.

6. For a succinct discussion of the necessity for control groups in manpower research, see Michael E. Borus and William R. Tash, MEASURING THE IMPACTS OF MANPOWER PROGRAMS (Ann Arbor: Institute of Labor & Industrial Relations, 1970), pp. 15-20.

7. Glen G. Cain and Robinson G. Hollister, "The Methodology of Evaluating Social Action Programs," in PUBLIC-PRIVATE MANPOWER POLICIES, Arnold R. Weber, et al., eds., Industrial Relations Research Association, 1969, p. 11.

8. Downs, BUREAUCRACY, p. 269.

9. Such an approach is relatively unfamiliar to economists, whose data bases are (1) frequently so large that the effect of outliers is very small, and (2) so impenetrable that identifying outliers is of no use since the cause of their deviance cannot be ascertained.

10. H.E. Freeman and C.C. Sherwood, "Research in Large-Scale Intervention Programs," THE JOURNAL OF SOCIAL ISSUES 21, no. 1, January 1965, pp. 11-28.

11. D.T. Campbell and J.C. Stanley, EXPERIMENTAL AND QUASI-EXPERIMENTAL DESIGNS FOR RESEARCH (Chicago: Rand-McNally, 1966).

12. These performance measures were taken from those shown in Table 2-2. The comparison cities were not required to report the data corresponding to many of the measures.

13. It was interesting to find that although the 1970 unemployment was different between the two groups, the 1970 to 1971 change in unemployment was not.

14. Shulberg and Baker (1968), "Program Evaluation Models."

15. We strongly recommend that the reader examine the sections of Chapter 3 headed "Introduction," "Recommendations," "Findings Concerning Program Goals," and "Conclusions," as well as Appendix 2, for a more complete understanding of how we arrived at our conclusions.

16. Weiss and Rein speak to the same issue: "Communities which apply for action program funds differ systematically from communities which do not apply and communities accepted for funding are almost always a rationally selected subset of the applicants." Weiss and Rein (1970), "Evaluation."

17. We strongly recommend that the reader examine Chapter 3, and also Appendix 2 for a more complete understanding of how we arrived at our conclusions.

18. Freeman and Sherwood, "Intervention Programs."

Appendix 2
Definitions and Job Bank City Characteristics

1. Public Employment Service Offices in several cities have adopted a new organizational arrangement known as the "Conceptual Model" (COMO). Employment Service operations are quite different in these cities than elsewhere.

Glossary

ADP	Automated Data Processing
ASM(1)	Assistant Secretary of Labor for Manpower, from beginning of study to July 3, 1970.
ASM(2)	Assistant Secretary of Labor for Manpower, from July 3, 1970 to end of study.
BOB	Bureau of the Budget
CA	Community Agency
COMO	Comprehensive Manpower Services Model
DMMS	Division of Manpower Matching Systems
DOL	Department of Labor
DPOA	Division of Program Data Analysis
ES	Employment Service
ESARS	Employment Service Automated Reporting System
FAP	Family Assistance Plan
ICESA	Interstate Conference of Employment Security Administrators
JBOR	Job Bank Operations Review
LLA	Chief, Division of Manpower Matching Systems, Manpower Administration.
MA	Manpower Administration
MDTA	Manpower Development and Training Act
MLA	Director, Office in which Division of Manpower Matching Systems was located.
MLR-OPER	Director, Office and Research and Development, Manpower Administration
OMB	Office of Management and Budget
OMMDS	Office of Manpower Management Data Systems
OTS	Office of Technical Support
PIP	Phased Implementation Progression for Computer-Assisted Manpower Operations Network.
SMSA	Standard Metropolitan Statistical Area.
USES or USTES	United States Employment Service.
ULA	Director, U.S. Training and Employment Service.
ULR-OPER	Director, Office in which Office of Research and Development was located.
VER	Veteran's Employment Representative.
WIN	Work Incentive Program.

Index

Index

About the Authors

Joseph C. Ullman is Associate Professor in the Krannert Graduate School of Industrial Administration, Purdue University, Lafayette, Indiana. He has also taught at the University of Chicago and at Florida International University. During the 1969-70 academic year, he worked as a Manpower Analyst at the U.S. Department of Labor on a Brookings Institution Economic Policy Fellowship. He has served as a consultant on labor market and manpower information system problems to Auerbach Corporation, Inland Steel Corporation and the U.S. Department of Labor. He was an Associate of the National Manpower Policy Task Force for several years. He has written widely on manpower, labor market information and industrial relations topics.

George P. Huber is Professor in the Graduate School of Business, the Department of Industrial Engineering, and the Industrial Relations Research Institute at the University of Wisconsin in Madison. He teaches and conducts research in the areas of administrative decision-making, organization design, and research and evaluation methodology. He has taught at the University of Missouri and Purdue University, in addition to the three departments of the University of Wisconsin. He has held full-time positions with Emerson Electric Manufacturing Co., Proctor and Gamble Co., and the U.S. Department of Labor. He has served as a consultant in decision-making and research methods to the U.S. Department of Labor, Wisconsin Regional Medical Project, and the Wisconsin Department of Labor, Industry and Human Relations. He has served through the auspices of a consulting firm as a consultant to the U.S. Navy and the U.S. Department of Defense.